# TRILLION DOLLAR COACH

ALSO BY THE AUTHORS

*How Google Works*

ALSO BY ERIC SCHMIDT

*The New Digital Age: Reshaping the Future of People,*
*Nations, and Business* (coauthored with Jared Cohen)

# TRILLION DOLLAR COACH

The Leadership Playbook of
Silicon Valley's Bill Campbell

ERIC SCHMIDT

JONATHAN ROSENBERG

AND ALAN EAGLE

HARPER
BUSINESS

*An Imprint of* HarperCollins*Publishers*

HarperCollins books may be purchased for educational, business, or sales promotional use. For information, please email the Special Markets Department at SPsales@harpercollins.com.

FIRST EDITION

Library of Congress Cataloging-in-Publication Data

Names: Schmidt, Eric, 1955 April 27– author. | Rosenberg, Jonathan, 1961– author. | Eagle, Alan, author.
Title: Trillion dollar coach : the leadership playbook of Silicon Valley's Bill Campbell / Eric Schmidt, Jonathan Rosenberg and Alan Eagle.
Description: First edition. | New York, NY : HarperBusiness, [2019] | Includes bibliographical references and index.
Identifiers: LCCN 2018041400 | ISBN 9780062839268 (hardcover)
Subjects: LCSH: Employees—Coaching of. | Management. | Mentoring in business. | Campbell, Bill, 1940–2016—Anecdotes. | Business consultants—United States—Biography. | Executives—United States—Biography. | Santa Clara Valley (Santa Clara County, Calif.)—Biography—Anecdotes.
Classification: LCC HF5549.5.C53 S375 2019 | DDC 658.4/07124—dc23 LC record available at https://lccn.loc.gov/2018041400

19 20 21 22 23   LSC   10 9 8 7 6 5 4 3 2 1

TO BILL

# CONTENTS

# Foreword

Nearly a decade ago, I read a story in *Fortune* about Silicon Valley's best-kept secret. It wasn't a piece of hardware or a bit of software. It wasn't even a product. It was a man. His name was Bill Campbell, and he wasn't a hacker. He was a football coach turned sales guy. Yet somehow, Bill had become so influential that he went on a weekly Sunday walk with Steve Jobs, and the Google founders said they wouldn't have made it without him.

Bill's name sounded familiar, but I couldn't place it. Eventually it hit me: I recognized him from a case I had taught a few times on a management dilemma at Apple in the mid-1980s, when a brave, bright young manager named Donna Dubinsky challenged a distribution plan from Steve Jobs himself. Bill Campbell was Donna's boss's boss, and he dished out exactly the kind of tough love you'd expect from a football coach: he tore her proposal apart, pushed her to come up with something stronger, and then stood up for her. I hadn't heard of him since—the next few decades of his career were a mystery.

The story gave me a clue about why: Bill loved shining the spotlight on others but preferred to stay in the shadows himself. I was writing a book on how helping others can drive our success, and it dawned on me that he would be a fascinating character to profile. But how do you profile someone who shuns public attention?

I started by cobbling together everything I could find about him online. I learned that what Bill lacked in physical strength, he made up for in heart. He was the MVP of his high school football team despite standing five feet ten and weighing 165 pounds. When the track coach was short on hurdlers, Bill volunteered. Since he couldn't jump high enough to clear the hurdles, he just ran right through them, bruising himself all the way to the regional championships. In college he played football at Columbia, where he was elected captain, and he went on to become the head coach there, struggling through six straight losing seasons. His Achilles' heel? He cared too much about his players. He was reluctant to bench walk-ons who gave it their all and refused to ask his stars to put sports above school. He was there to make his players successful in life, not on the field. He was more interested in their well-being than in winning.

When Bill decided to transition to business, it was his old football teammates who opened the door. They were convinced that his weakness in a zero-sum sport could be a strength in many companies. Sure enough, Bill ended up excelling as an executive at Apple and as the CEO of Intuit. Every time I talked to someone in Silicon Valley who had a reputation for unusual generosity, they told me the same thing: it was Bill Campbell who gave them their worldview. Not wanting to bother Bill himself, I started reaching out to his mentees. Soon I had a flurry of calls with Bill's protégés, who described him as a father and compared him to Oprah. The calls usually ended with me scribbling down a dozen new names of people whose lives Bill had changed. One of those names was Jonathan Rosenberg, one of the authors of this book.

When I got in touch with Jonathan in 2012, he took the liberty of copying Bill himself on the email thread. Bill declined to be featured, closing the door on that chapter of my book—and on my quest to find out how he had done so much good for others while doing great for himself as well. Ever since, I've wondered how he flourished as a giver in a field that supposedly rewards takers, and what we could learn from him about leadership and management.

I'm delighted to say that at long last, thanks to this book, I have my answers. *Trillion Dollar Coach* reveals that to be a great manager, you have to be a great coach. After all, the higher you climb, the more your success depends on making other people successful. By definition, that's what coaches do.

For the past ten years, I've had the privilege of teaching the core teamwork and leadership class at Wharton. The course is based on rigorous research, and I'm struck by how brilliantly Bill Campbell anticipated the evidence. He was living theories in the 1980s that experts didn't even develop (let alone validate) until decades later. I was also taken aback by how many of Bill's insights around managing people and coaching teams are still ripe for systematic study.

Bill was ahead of his time. The lessons of his experience are timely in a collaborative world, where the fates of our careers and our companies hinge on the quality of our relationships. But I believe they're also timeless: Bill's approach to coaching would work in any era.

Coaching is in vogue: it used to be just athletes and entertainers who had coaches, but now we have leaders taking on executive coaches and employees learning from speaking coaches. The reality, though, is that a formal coach will see only a fraction of the moments where you could benefit from feedback and guidance. It's up to all of us to coach our employees, our colleagues, and even sometimes our bosses.

I've come to believe that coaching might be even more essential than mentoring to our careers and our teams. Whereas mentors dole out words of wisdom, coaches roll up their sleeves and get their hands dirty. They don't just believe in our potential; they get in the arena to help us realize our potential. They hold up a mirror so we can see our blind spots and they hold us accountable for working through our sore spots. They take responsibility for making us better without taking credit for our accomplishments. And I can't think of a better role model for a coach than Bill Campbell.

I don't make that statement lightly. I've had the chance to learn up close from some elite coaches—not just in business, but in sports, too. As a springboard diver, I trained under Olympic coaches, and more recently as an organizational psychologist, I've worked with great coaches like Brad Stevens of the Boston Celtics. Bill Campbell doesn't just belong in that elite group of world-class coaches. He invented his own category, because he could coach people doing work he didn't even understand.

In 2012, the same year that I gave up on writing about Bill, I was invited to give a talk at a global Google event on how I would run the company as an organizational psychologist. Having worked for a few years with Google's pioneering people analytics team, it became obvious to me that almost everything great in the company happened in teams. That was my pitch in the talk: start treating teams, not individuals, as the fundamental building block of the organization. My Google colleagues did one better: they launched a major study, which they published as Project Aristotle, to identify the distinguishing characteristics of their most successful teams.

The five key factors could have been taken right out of Bill Campbell's playbook. Excellent teams at Google had psychological safety (people knew that if they took risks, their manager would have their back). The teams had clear goals, each role was meaningful, and members were reliable and confident that the team's mission would make a difference. You'll see that Bill was a master at establishing those conditions: he went to extraordinary lengths to build safety, clarity, meaning, dependability, and impact into each team he coached.

Sheryl Sandberg and I have often lamented that every bookstore has a self-help section, but there isn't a help-others section. *Trillion Dollar Coach* belongs in the help-others section: it's a guide for bringing out the best in others, for being simultaneously supportive and challenging, and for giving more than lip service to the notion of putting people first.

What's most remarkable about Bill Campbell's story is that the more you read about him, the more you'll see opportunities every day for becoming more like him. There are small choices, like treating everyone you meet with dignity and respect. And there are bigger commitments, like taking the time to show a sincere interest in the lives of your team—to the point of remembering where their kids go to school.

Bill Campbell didn't need or want the glory of being profiled in a book, let alone being the subject of an entire book. But for a man who lived his life by giving his knowledge away, open-sourcing his secrets strikes me as a fitting tribute.

—Adam Grant

# TRILLION DOLLAR COACH

——————

# CHAPTER 1

# The Caddie and the CEO

On a warm April day in 2016, a large crowd gathered on the football field at Sacred Heart School, in the heart of Atherton, California, to honor William Vincent Campbell, Jr., who had recently succumbed to cancer at the age of seventy-five. Bill had been a transcendent figure in the technology business since moving west in 1983, playing a critical role in the success of Apple, Google, Intuit, and numerous other companies. To say he was tremendously respected would be a gross understatement—loved is more like it. Among the audience that day were dozens of technology leaders—Larry Page. Sergey Brin. Mark Zuckerberg. Sheryl Sandberg. Tim Cook. Jeff Bezos. Mary Meeker. John Doerr. Ruth Porat. Scott Cook. Brad Smith. Ben Horowitz. Marc Andreessen. Such a concentration of industry pioneers and power is rarely seen, at least not in Silicon Valley.

We—Jonathan Rosenberg and Eric Schmidt—sat among the audience, making subdued small talk, soft sunshine contrasting with the somber mood. We had both worked closely with Bill in the previous fifteen years, since we had joined Google as the CEO (Eric, in 2001) and the head of products (Jonathan, in 2002). Bill had been our coach, meeting with us individually every week or two to talk through the various challenges we had faced as we helped grow the company. He had guided us as individuals and teammates, working mostly behind the scenes as Google went from a quirky startup to one of the most valuable companies and brands in the world. Without Bill's help, there was a chance that none of that would have happened. We called him Coach, but we also called him friend, and in this we were like pretty much everyone around us. In fact, as we later found out, many of the people in the audience that day, an audience that numbered well over a thousand people, considered Bill to be their *best* friend. So who, among all of these best friends, would have the honor of eulogizing our Coach? Which high-tech luminary would step to the podium?

## THE CHAMPION FROM HOMESTEAD

Bill Campbell didn't even get to California until his early forties, and he had started his business career only a few years before that. In fact, this Silicon Valley success story packed a few lifetimes' worth of accomplishments into his seventy-five-year span. He grew up pugnacious and smart in the western Pennsylvania steel town of Homestead, where his father taught physical education in the local high school and moonlighted at the mill. Bill was a good student and worked hard. Astute too: he wrote an April 1955 op-ed in his school newspaper that reminded his fellow students "there is nothing more important to you in later life" than good grades. "Loafing in school may prevent one's chances of success." He was a freshman at the time.

A football star at Homestead High, Bill left home in the fall of 1958 to attend Columbia University in Manhattan. He was an unlikely-looking football hero even in that era when football players were far more human-sized than they are today: maybe five ten, 165 pounds (although listed in the program at 180). But he quickly earned the respect of coaches and teammates alike with his all-out play and on-field intelligence. By his senior year, the fall of 1961, Bill was the captain of the team, playing practically every minute of every game as a linebacker on defense and lineman (guard) on offense. He earned All-Ivy honors and helped lead the team to the Ivy League title, the only one in Columbia's history. The team's coach, the wonderfully named Buff Donelli, called Bill "a tremendous influence" in winning the title. "If he stood 6 feet 2 and weighed 225 pounds and played pro ball, he'd be the greatest lineman the league ever had, a ball of fire. But he's a little guy who weighs only 162. Not even in college ball do you find guards that small. Ordinarily you can't play football with little guys. Attitude generally isn't enough. A coach needs attitude plus players."[1]

Bill's attitude, naturally, was all about the team, saying

that it succeeded "because the players worked together and had senior leadership."[2]

## TOO MUCH COMPASSION

Bill didn't have much money, so he helped pay for his education at Columbia by driving a cab. He learned the city so well that later in life he often argued with his longtime driver and friend, Scotty Kramer, about the best route to take. (When it came to navigating New York you didn't question the coach,

Bill (67) leads the blocking for Columbia during the Lions' 26–14 victory over Harvard on October 21, 1961.[3]

Scotty says.) He graduated from Columbia in 1962 with a degree in economics, received a master's degree in education in 1964, and migrated north to become an assistant football coach at Boston College. Bill was an outstanding coach and quickly became highly respected among his peers. So when his alma mater, Columbia, asked him to return as its head coach in 1974, he agreed. Although Columbia's football program was woeful, Bill's loyalty guided him back to Manhattan.

(One of Bill's coaching colleagues, Jim Rudgers, notes that before Bill "let his heart take him" back to Columbia, he was considered one of the top assistant coaches in the country

Bill's teammates carry him off the field after Columbia's 37–6 win over University of Pennsylvania on November 18, 1961. The victory clinched Columbia's first Ivy League championship.[4]

and was offered the opportunity to coach at Penn State under Joe Paterno. At the time, Paterno was one of the top coaches in the country, and it seems likely that Bill would have continued to thrive as a coach had he joined the Nittany Lions. In fact, this book might have been about Bill Campbell, college football legend, rather than Bill Campbell, Silicon Valley legend. And to learn more about him you might be doing a Yahoo or Bing search!)

Despite his abundant coaching talent, Bill did not win in his return to Columbia. Hampered by crummy facilities that were at least a thirty-minute bus ride from campus in afternoon traffic, an administration that was perhaps not fully committed to gridiron success, and a city in general decline, the Lions won only twelve games during his tenure, losing forty-one. His most hopeful season was 1978, when the team started 3-1-1 but then got crushed at Giants Stadium, 69–0, by a much bigger (physically and numerically) Rutgers squad. Bill decided partway through the 1979 campaign that he was going to resign. He completed the season and was done.

Bill worked so hard during his time at Columbia that at one point he had to take a break in a hospital to recover from exhaustion. Recruiting players was particularly challenging. Bill later said that he would have to visit a hundred prospects just to get twenty-five of them to come. "I'd leave after workout programs, at 4:30, and I'd drive to Albany and back in a night. Scranton and back," he added. "Just so I could be back in the office the next day."[5]

His failure, though, wasn't for lack of players. It was, according to Bill, for too much compassion. "There is something that I would say is called dispassionate toughness that you need [as a football coach], and I don't think I have it. What you need to do is not worry about feelings. You've got to push everybody and everything harder and be almost insensitive about feelings. You replace a kid with another kid; you take an older guy and replace him with a younger guy. That is the nature of the game. Survival of the fittest. The best players play. In my case, I worried about that. I tried to make sure the kids understood what we were doing. I just think I wasn't hard-edged enough."[6]

Bill may have been correct in believing that success as a football coach depends on "dispassion," but in business there is growing evidence that compassion is a key factor to success.[*7] And as it turned out, this notion of bringing compassion to the team worked much better for Bill in the business world than on the football field.

## LET'S RUN IT

His football career was done. At age thirty-nine, Bill entered the business world by taking a job with the ad agency J. Walter Thompson. He started in Chicago, supporting Kraft, then several months later moved back to New York to support Kodak. He dove into his job with customary passion, impressing his clients in Rochester, New York, so much with his

---

* A 2006 paper by Peter Frost, Jane Dutton, Sally Maitlis, Jacoba Lilius, Jason Kanov, and Monica Worline contains a compendium of research over the past century confirming the high value of compassion in the workplace and organizations.

knowledge and insights about their business that they soon hired him away from the agency. Bill rose quickly at Kodak, and by 1983 he was working in London as the company's head of consumer products for Europe. During his initial job search in 1979, one of his Columbia football buddies had connected Bill with John Sculley, who was then a senior executive at PepsiCo. Bill didn't take the job that John offered at Pepsi, but in 1983 Sculley decamped to Silicon Valley to become CEO of Apple, and shortly thereafter he gave Bill a call. Would he be willing to leave Kodak and move his young family—he had married the former Roberta Spagnola, a dean at Columbia, in 1976—west to come to Apple?

"My career had been blunted by a lot of years as a dumbass football coach," Bill later said. "I felt that because of my background, I would always be below my peer group and trying to catch up. Going out to the wild, woolly west, where it was more a meritocracy, I would have a chance to move quickly and sit on the management team."[8] Move quickly, indeed. Within nine months of joining Apple, Bill was promoted to VP of sales and marketing and given the task of overseeing the launch of the highly anticipated Macintosh, Apple's new computer that would replace the Apple II as the company's flagship product.

To kick off the launch, the company made a big move: it bought a slot to run a commercial during the Super Bowl, which would be played in Tampa, Florida, on January 22, 1984. Once the ad was produced, Bill and the team showed it to Apple cofounder Steve Jobs. An allusion to George Orwell's novel *1984*, it showed a young woman running through a dark hallway, fleeing guards, and emerging into a chamber where hundreds of gray-clad, head-shaven men are listening, zombie-like, to a droning "big brother" figure on a large screen before them. With a yell, she throws a large mallet through the screen, causing it to explode. A narrator promises that the Apple Macintosh will show us why "1984 won't be like *1984*."*

Steve loved the ad. E. Floyd Kvamme, Bill's boss at the time, loved the ad. Bill loved the ad. About ten days before the game, they showed it to the board.

The board hated the ad. This is terrible, was the universal opinion, too costly and too controversial. They wanted to know if they could sell the airtime to some other advertiser. Was it too late to back out? A couple of days later, one of the Apple sales executives told Bill and Floyd that she had been able to find a buyer for the slot. "What do you think we should do?" Floyd asked Bill.

"Fuck it! Let's run it," was Bill's response. They never told the board or other top executives that they had a potential buyer for the slot, and ran the ad. It became not only the most popular spot of the game, but one of the most famous commercials of all time, ushering in the era of Super Bowl ads becoming as big as the game itself. A *Los Angeles Times* column in 2017 called it the "only great Super Bowl commercial ever."[9] Not bad for a "dumb-ass football coach" less than five years removed from his final season.

In 1987, Apple decided to spin off a separate software company called Claris and offered Bill the position of CEO.

---

* Search "Apple 1984 commercial" on your favorite search engine to see the ad.

He jumped at the opportunity. Claris did well, but by 1990 Apple pulled it back into the fold as a subsidiary rather than follow the original plan of letting it become its own public company. This shift spurred Bill and several other Claris executives to leave. It was an emotional decision, and when Bill departed, several Claris employees demonstrated their gratitude to him by taking out a full-page ad in the *San Jose Mercury News*. "So long, Coach," the headline read. "Bill, we'll miss your leadership, your vision, your wisdom, your friendship and your spirit . . ." the ad continued. "You taught us how to stand on our own. You built us to last. And even though you're no longer coaching our team, we're going to do our best to keep making you proud." Claris continued as an Apple subsidiary until 1998.

Bill became the CEO of a startup named GO Corporation, which attempted to create the world's first pen-based handheld computer (a precursor to the PalmPilot and today's smartphones). It was an ambitious vision but ahead of its time, and the company shut down in 1994. "GO didn't go," Bill was fond of saying.

Around that time, Intuit cofounder and CEO Scott Cook, along with his board of directors, was looking to replace himself as CEO. John Doerr, a Kleiner Perkins venture capitalist,* introduced Bill to Scott. At first, the founder wasn't impressed with the coach. A couple of months passed and Scott still didn't have a new CEO, so he agreed to meet

---

* John is one of the more successful VCs in Silicon Valley, having led Kleiner Perkins's investments in companies such as Google, Amazon, Netscape, Sun, Intuit, and Compaq.

San Jose Mercury News ■ Monday, February 25, 1991  **5D**

# So long, Coach.

Claris has just lost one of our hardest-working employees.

Bill Campbell is on his way to lead another bunch of impossible dreamers over at GO Corporation, those guys with the pen-based notebook computing system.

And the bunch he left behind would like to publicly tender him the biggest compliment we can conjure:

Bill, we'll miss your leadership, your vision, your wisdom, your friendship and your spirit.

But–thanks to all of the above–we're going to be fine without you.

In 1987, when Apple decided to get out of the software business, you volunteered to start a spin-off company.

You began with a handful of nearly-free Apple software products, a few rebels, a name, "Claris," and built us into the world's leading Mac software company.

We just finished our best quarter ever in sales, profits, market share and growth.

You taught us how to stand on our own.

You built us to last.

And even though you're no longer coaching our team, we're going to do our best to keep making you proud.

CLARIS

Chris Gaede

11

with Bill again. They went on a walk around a neighborhood in Palo Alto, California, and this time the two clicked.
"The first time we met, we talked about business and strategy," Scott says. "But when we talked again, we got off
of strategy and talked instead about leadership and people.
The other people I had interviewed had a cookie-cutter approach to developing people. You can have any color you
want as long as it's black. But Bill, he was a technicolor
rainbow. He appreciated that each person had a different
story and background. He was so nuanced and different in
how he approached growth challenges and leadership challenges. I was looking for a way to grow our people in a way
I couldn't. Bill was great at that."

In 1994, Bill became Intuit's CEO. He shepherded the
company through several years of growth and success, stepping down in 2000.* Although he did not know it at the time,
he was about to enter the third chapter of his career, a return
to coaching full-time, but not on a football field.

When Steve Jobs was forced out of Apple in 1985, Bill
Campbell was one of the few leaders at the company who
fought against the move. Dave Kinser, an Apple colleague of
Bill's at the time, recalls Bill saying that "we've got to keep
Steve in the company. He's way too talented to just let him
leave!" Steve remembered that loyalty. When he returned to
Apple and became its CEO in 1997, and most of the board

---

* Bill stepped down as Intuit CEO in July 1998, then returned to the
position in September 1999, when his replacement, Bill Harris, decided to
resign. Bill stayed on as CEO until early 2000.

members stepped down, Steve named Bill as one of the new directors.* (Bill served on the Apple board until 2014.)

Steve and Bill became close friends, speaking frequently and spending many Sunday afternoons walking around their Palo Alto neighborhood discussing all sorts of topics. Bill became a sounding board for Steve on a wide variety of subjects, a coach, mentor, and friend. But Steve was not Bill's only coachee. In fact, even though he left football in 1979, "the Coach" never stopped coaching. He was always available to chat with friends, neighbors, colleagues, fellow parents from his kids' school; he'd give them a hug, listen to whatever was going on, and usually spin some story that helped them gain some perspective, draw some insight, or make a decision.

So when Bill stepped down as Intuit's CEO in 2000 (he remained as chairman until 2016) and was looking for his next challenge, John Doerr invited him to come to Kleiner Perkins, the venerable venture capital firm, and become a coach for its portfolio companies. Venture firms often have "entrepreneurs in residence," bright, usually young, technologists who work at the firms while they noodle over their next big idea. Why not have an executive in residence, John thought, someone who was seasoned in operations and strategy, to help the firm's startups through the ups and downs of growth (or lack thereof)? Bill agreed and settled into life on Sand Hill Road.

---

* Technically, Steve was the "interim CEO" of Apple from 1997 until January 2000, when he dropped "interim" from his title.

## THE GOOGLE COACH

One day in 2001 a local startup, run by a couple of brash kids from Stanford, decided to bring in a "professional" CEO: Eric Schmidt. Eric built the software operations at Sun Microsystems and served as CEO and chairman at Novell. John Doerr advised Eric that he needed Bill Campbell as his coach. Eric had met Bill when Sun CEO Scott McNealy tried to hire him and was impressed with his accomplishments and energy. Once, when Bill came into the Sun offices for a meeting, he remarked that he had just returned from a one-day trip to Japan! This made a huge impression on Eric.

But still, Eric was a rightfully proud man and Doerr's suggestion offended him. By that time, Eric was already a big deal: CEO of Novell, former CTO of Sun, MS and PhD in computer science from Cal, and BS from Princeton. That's a lot of letters; what could this gruff guy from Pennsylvania—an ex-football coach!—have to teach him?

A lot, it turns out. In less than a year, Eric's self-review showed how much he had come around: "Bill Campbell has been very helpful in coaching all of us," he wrote. "In hindsight, his role was needed from the beginning. I should have encouraged this structure sooner, ideally the moment I started at Google."

For fifteen years, Bill met with Eric just about every week. And not only Eric: Bill became a coach to Jonathan, Larry Page, and several other Google leaders. He attended Eric's staff meeting every week and was a frequent presence on the company's Mountain View, California, campus (which, conveniently, was a stone's throw from the Intuit campus, where Bill was still chairman).

For those fifteen years, Bill's counsel was deeply influential. It's not that he told us what to do—far from it. If Bill had opinions about product and strategy, he usually kept them to himself. But he made sure the team was communicating, that tensions and disagreements were brought to the surface and discussed, so that when the big decisions were made, everyone was on board, whether they agreed or not. We can say, without a doubt, that Bill Campbell was one of the people most integral to Google's success. Without him, the company would not be where it is today.

Which would be enough for just about anyone, but not Bill. While he was working with Google's senior team and with Steve Jobs at Apple, he was also helping so many more. He coached Brad Smith, former CEO of Intuit. He coached John Donahoe, former CEO of eBay. He coached former U.S. Vice President Al Gore. He coached Dick Costolo, former CEO of Twitter. He coached Mike McCue, CEO of Flipboard. He coached Donna Dubinsky, CEO of Numenta. He coached Nirav Tolia, CEO of Nextdoor. He coached Lee C. Bollinger, president of Columbia University. He coached Shellye Archambeau, former CEO of MetricStream. He coached Ben Horowitz, partner at venture capital firm Andreessen Horowitz. He coached the boys and girls flag football teams at Sacred Heart. He coached Bill Gurley, general partner at venture capital firm Benchmark. He coached NFL Hall of Famer Ronnie Lott. He coached Danny Shader, CEO of Handle Financial. He coached Sundar Pichai, CEO of Google.

He coached Dan Rosensweig, CEO of Chegg. He coached Charlie Batch, fellow Homestead native and former quarterback for the Pittsburgh Steelers. He coached Jesse Rogers, managing director of Altamont Capital Partners. He coached John Hennessy, former president of Stanford University. He coached Sheryl Sandberg, COO of Facebook.

## BALLSY AND BRUNO

And when it came time to eulogize Bill at his memorial, none of those people took the podium. In fact, the first person who stepped to the microphone that day was Bill's college football teammate Lee Black. Lee started talking about his friend "Ballsy," who we quickly figured out was none other than Bill.

When Bill showed up at Columbia, he was the smallest guy on the team, but he proved to be the most pugnacious in tackling and blocking drills. He'd get knocked down time after time, then get back up and do it again. One day, they were riding on the bus to practice when Lee said, "Campbell, you have more balls than a brass monkey." Everyone on the team had nicknames, and thereafter "Ballsy" was Bill's. Even when he was named the captain of the team his senior season, he was never Captain, always Ballsy. Indeed, the Campbell Sports Center at Columbia, which houses a strength and conditioning space, meeting rooms for student athletes, and offices for coaches, is sometimes referred to as "Balls Hall," at least within the football community.

We learned a lot about Bill that day, but nothing more

surprising than the fact that this great business leader, this CEO, Steve Jobs confidant, Ivy League champion, Columbia football coach and chairman of the board, father of two and stepfather of three,* had earned the honorific "Ballsy" through his aggressive play on the Columbia football field. Besides his Columbia teammates, no one else had heard Bill's nickname. But it made sense.

In the audience were people from many different walks of life. Scotty Kramer, Bill's longtime New York driver and buddy, made the trip to California, as did Danny Collins, a head waiter at one of Bill's favorite New York restaurants, Smith & Wollensky. Jim Rudgers, a retired college football coach who worked with Bill at Columbia and at whose wedding Bill served as best man, hates flying, but there was no way he was going to miss Bill's service, so he drove across the country from Rhode Island. There were Bill's Columbia football clan, men he had played with, men he had coached. There were the Stanford football players who lived at the Campbell home during summers. There was the staff from the Old Pro, the Palo Alto sports bar that Bill co-owned and frequented. There were the friends Bill took on his annual Super Bowl trip, the friends he took on his annual Cabo trip, and the friends he took on his annual baseball trip to Pittsburgh and other eastern locales. Because this was not a gathering of professionals who sort of knew Bill and came to pay their respects and network. This was a gathering of people who loved Bill.

---

* Bill and Roberta divorced in 2009. He married Eileen Bocci in 2015.

Among them was Bruno Fortozo, Bill's regular caddie at the El Dorado golf course in Cabo San Lucas, where Bill played when he visited his vacation home there. Bill, Bruno, and their families had become friends over the years, enjoying plenty of banter on the course and dinners together at restaurants around Cabo. "Most of the guests, you don't cross the line with them," Bruno says. "But Bill, he was such a happy guy. He was nice to every single person."

Bill had hosted Bruno, along with his wife and sons, at his homes in Palo Alto and Montana when the Fortozo clan came north for vacation a few years before. So there was no way Bruno was going to miss Bill's memorial. When he arrived at Sacred Heart that afternoon, he was ushered toward the front, close to Bill's family. "I was sitting right behind Mr. Cook and Eddy Cue, from Apple," he says. "And right next to a guy, I forget his name. I think he runs Google."

Bill Campbell was known for many things, but perhaps his most notable characteristic, his signature, was the hug. Bill hugged everybody. In fact, when Microsoft announced its proposed acquisition of Intuit at a public event in October 1994, Bill strode across the stage and gave Bill Gates (not noted for his hugging skills) a big hug. (The deal later fell apart. Causality between the hug and the deal failure has never been proven.) Bill's was never a wimpy, lean-in, don't-really-mean-it, let's-not-upset-the-lawyers, pat-on-the-back hug with a couple of air kisses thrown in. Nope, he was a bear when it came to hugging. He hugged you like he meant it, because he did. As Lee neared the end of his remarks, he looked out at the audience and invited them to do Bill proud and hug the people around them.

Which is how Larry Page, the cofounder of Google and CEO of Alphabet, came to be hugging Bruno Fortozo, the caddie from Cabo San Lucas. "Mr. Campbell treats everyone the same way," Bruno says. "I didn't know who all the people were around me, they were all just friends of Bill." Which is as good a tribute to Bill as any of the other words spoken that day.

Lee was followed by Pat Gallagher. Pat is a highly accomplished person, a former longtime senior executive with the San Francisco Giants and one of the most admired sports business minds in the country. His thirty-three years with the Giants ended in 2009, a departure, he says, that led directly to the team winning World Series titles in 2010, 2012, and 2014. But he wasn't given the honor of eulogizing Bill through résumé or pedigree. He earned the honor through friendship. He and Bill had been neighbors in Palo Alto, meeting shortly after Bill and Roberta moved west in the mid-1980s, and built a friendship the way neighbors of a similar ilk do: coaching youth sports together, gathering with team families after games at beer and burger joints, playing with kids at the park, taking walks around the neighborhood, and having spontaneous dinner parties. Friends who stay true through many ups and a few downs.

As Pat said that day, "Most of us have a circle of friends and acquaintances in our lives that come and go through the years. And then we have a much smaller subset of our close friends and our family. And then an even smaller number, maybe enough to count on one or two fingers, our best friends. Best friends are the ones who you can talk to about anything and you don't have to worry. You know they will always be there. Bill Campbell was my best friend. I know that there are only about two thousand other people who also considered Bill to be their best friends, too. But, I was okay with that because somehow Bill found the time for each one of us. He had the same twenty-four-hour days that the rest of us have, but somehow he found the time to always be there for everyone on that list. It didn't matter to Bill where you were on the list of friends. He would always be there for you no matter what."

As the memorial came to a close and people milled around and chatted, Philipp Schindler sought out Eric. Philipp runs the business side of Google and was one of the Googlers who had been influenced by Bill for several years. Just a few weeks earlier, Philipp had attended a training seminar at Google where Bill was teaching his management principles to a group of Google execs so that they could pass them on to the company's next generation. Now Bill was gone, and Philipp wanted to help funnel his principles to others, not just at Google but to everyone. When he saw Eric, he asked him, Why don't we take the amazing wisdom Bill taught us and turn it into something we can share with the rest of the world? We have had the great privilege to work with a management legend. All of this could be lost if we don't do something.

# THE TRILLION
# DOLLAR COACH

Bill Campbell was a trillion dollar coach. In fact, a trillion dollars understates the value he created. He worked side by side with Steve Jobs to build Apple from near bankruptcy to a market capitalization of several hundred billion dollars. He worked side by side with Larry Page, Sergey Brin, and Eric to build Google (now Alphabet) from a startup to a market capitalization that's also several hundred billion dollars. So that's well over a trillion dollars already, and doesn't include the numerous other companies Bill advised. By that measure, Bill was the greatest executive coach the world has ever seen. And not an executive coach in the traditional mold, working solely to maximize the performance of individuals; Bill coached teams.

After Bill passed away, Google started teaching his principles via internal seminars to emerging leaders. So when, spurred by Philipp, we started to think about writing a book about Bill, we quickly rejected the idea of writing a hagiography.* After all, as Bill would have said (in more colorful language), who would want to read about the life of some dumb guy from Homestead, Pennsylvania? We don't know, but what we do know is that Bill's approach to coaching, both what he coached and how he coached it, was unique and incredibly—*a trillion dollars!*—successful. It is also

---

* A hagiography is a biography that idealizes the subject. Jonathan and Alan had to look it up when Eric told them that was not what we were going to write.

something needed in today's business world, when success lies in moving quickly and continually creating innovative new features, products, and services.

In our previous book, *How Google Works*, we argue that there is a new breed of employee, the smart creative, who is critical to achieving this speed and innovation. The smart creative is someone who combines technical depth with business savvy and creative flair. These people have always existed, but with the advent of the internet, smartphones, cloud computing, and all their attendant innovations, they can have a much greater impact than ever before. For companies to be successful, they must continually develop great products, and to do that they must attract smart creatives and build an environment where these employees can succeed at scale.

As we were researching this book and talking to the dozens of people Bill had coached in his career, we realized that this thesis misses an important piece of the business success puzzle. There is another, equally critical, factor for success in companies: teams that act as *communities*, integrating interests and putting aside differences to be individually and collectively obsessed with what's good for the company. Research shows that when people feel like they are part of a supportive community at work, they are more engaged with their jobs and more productive. Conversely, a lack of community is a leading factor in job burnout.[10]

But as anyone who has ever been a member of high-performance teams can tell you, teams don't always operate this way. Such teams are by their nature populated with smart, aggressive, ambitious, strong-willed, opinionated people with large egos. These people may work together, but they can also be rivals, competing for career advancement. Or if they are executives, they are often positioning their divisions or other organizational silos against each other—in "status conflicts"—to capture more resources and glory. People may want to rise to the next level, and it is awfully tempting to pursue that goal alongside or above the goal of team success. All too often, internal competition takes center stage, and compensation, bonuses, recognition, and even office size and location become the ways to keep score. This is problematic: in such an environment, selfish individuals can beat altruistic ones. This sort of "intragroup" conflict in teams will have, according to several studies (and common sense), negative effects on team outcomes.[11]

But teams of people who subordinate individual performance to that of the group will generally outperform teams that don't. The trick, then, is to corral any such "team of rivals" into a community and get them aligned in marching toward a common goal. A 2013 paper presents a set of "design principles" for doing this, such as developing strong mechanisms for making decisions and resolving conflicts.[12] But adhering to these principles is hard, and it gets even harder when you add in factors such as fast-moving industries, complex business models, technology-driven shifts, smart competitors, sky-high customer expectations, global expansion, demanding teammates . . . in other words, the reality of managing businesses today. As our colleague Patrick Pichette, Google's former CFO, puts it, when you have all of these factors in play *and* a team of ambitious, opinionated, competitive, smart people, there is tremendous "tension in the machine." This tension is a good thing; if you don't have it you will fade to irrelevance. But the tension makes it harder to cultivate community, and community is necessary to cultivate success.

To balance the tension and mold a team into a community, you need a coach, someone who works not only with individuals but also with the team as a whole to smooth out the constant tension, continuously nurture the community, and make sure it is aligned around a common vision and set of goals. Sometimes this coach may just work with the team leader, the executive in charge. But to be most effective—and this was Bill's model—the coach works with the entire team. At Google, Bill didn't just meet with Eric. He worked with Jonathan and several other people, and he attended Eric's staff meetings on a regular basis. This can be a hard thing for an executive to accept—having a "coach" getting involved in staff meetings and other things can seem like a sign of lack of confidence. A 2014 study finds that it is the most insecure managers who are threatened by suggestions from others (in other words, coaching). So, conversely, publicly accepting a coach can actually be a sign of confidence.[13] And a 2010 article notes that "group coaching" is effective but generally underused as a way to improve team or group performance (which the authors call "goal-focused change").[14]

At Google, Bill walked the halls and got to know people. His remit wasn't just about Eric and a few other individuals, it was about the team. He made the entire team better. When you think about what Bill accomplished, it's kind of amazing that there aren't more former sports coaches rising to prominence in the business world. There are plenty of books by athletic coaches offering lessons that go beyond sports, but not many successful sports coaches have found success as business operators. It was no accident that Bill Campbell spent the first decade of his career coaching football, perhaps the ultimate team sport. In football, when teammates don't work well together, not only does the team lose but people can get hurt. Over those years of playing and coaching, Bill learned that great teams need to work together, and he learned how to make that happen. Not just on the field, but in offices, hallways, and conference rooms. He came to master the art of identifying tensions among teammates and figuring out how to resolve them.

Every sports team needs a coach, and the best coaches make good teams great. The same goes in business: any company that wants to succeed in a time where technology has suffused every industry and most aspects of consumer life, where speed and innovation are paramount, must have team coaching as part of its culture. Coaching is the best way to mold effective people into powerful teams.

The problem is, it's not possible or practical to hire a coach for every team in a company, or even for just the executive teams. The questions are numerous: Where do you find the coaches? How much would that cost? More important, though, is that it just wouldn't work. As we talked to the dozens of people who had worked with Bill, something new and surprising started to emerge. Yes, Bill coached them, as he had coached us, on how to deal with numerous situations and challenges in their lives and businesses. But through that coaching he also showed them how to coach their people and teams, which made them much more effective managers and leaders. Time and time again, they note that whenever they face an interesting situation, they ask themselves, what would Bill do? And we realized, we do it, too. What would Bill do? How would the coach handle this situation?

It's not possible or practical to hire a coach for every team in the company, nor is it the right answer, because the best coach for any team is the manager who leads that team. Being a good coach is essential to being a good manager and leader. Coaching is no longer a specialty; you cannot be a good manager without being a good coach. You need to, according to a 1994 study, go beyond the "traditional notion of managing that focuses on controlling, supervising, evaluating and rewarding/punishing" to create a climate of communication, respect, feedback, and trust. All through coaching.[15]

Many of the other skills of management can be delegated, but not coaching. This is ultimately what Bill taught us. The path to success in a fast-moving, highly competitive, technology-driven business world is to form high-performing teams and give them the resources and freedom to do great things. And an essential component of high-performing teams is a leader who is both a savvy manager and a caring coach. At this, Bill Campbell was the best there ever was.

In this book we will examine both *what* Bill coached—what were the things he told people to do—and *how* he coached—what was his approach. We break the what and how into four sections: how Bill got the details right in management skills ranging from one-on-one and staff meetings to handling challenging employees; how he built trust with the people he worked with; how he built and created teams; and finally, how he made it okay to bring love into the workplace. Yes, you read that correctly: we said *love*. Where relevant, we refer to a selection of the many academic studies and articles that support Bill's techniques. Both the what and the how may seem so simple at first that they are practically aphorisms. But, as any experienced leader knows, they may be simple in concept, but they are hard in practice.[*16]

So hard, in fact, that as we were writing this book, we sometimes wondered if Bill was so unique that no one else could possibly combine the what and the how in the way that he did. Were we creating a "how to" manual to teach managers to be better coaches that only one person in the world, now, sadly, gone, could effectively use?

Our conclusion was no. There was only one Bill Campbell, perhaps the most extraordinary individual we have had the pleasure and honor to meet and befriend. But much of the what and the how of his coaching, we believe, can be replicated by others. If you are a manager, executive, or any other kind of leader of teams, in any kind of business or organization, you can be more effective and help your team perform better (and be happier) by becoming the coach of that team. Bill's principles have helped us and many others do that; we believe they can help you, too.

There was only one Coach Bill. But this book, we hope,

---

* A 2010 study from Curtin University of Technology in Perth, Australia, includes several failure modes for managers acting as coaches, including not taking enough time, believing that people can't be developed, and a perception that coaching isn't aligned with bottom-line results.

captures his insights in a way that makes them available to current and future leaders, so those leaders can benefit from his wisdom and humanity as much as the people who knew him did. As Ben Horowitz puts it, "You don't want to channel Bill, because no one can be him. But I learned from him how to get better: a higher level of honesty, a better understanding of people and management."

## DON'T F*** IT UP

In writing this book, we interviewed dozens of people whose lives have been profoundly touched by Bill in one way or another. Boyhood friends, Columbia teammates, players he coached at Boston College and Columbia, fellow football coaches, colleagues at Kodak, Apple, Claris, GO, and Intuit, business executives he coached, Stanford players who regularly crashed at his Palo Alto home, family, friends, and even kids at Sacred Heart he coached as middle schoolers on the flag football team. Many of them got choked up at some point in their interview. Bill created that level of love and devotion in the people whose lives he touched. We have been entrusted with a legacy and know that this book matters to those who loved Bill.

Bill was a delightfully profane man. He used the F-word the way people today use *like*, almost as if it's a new part of speech, not verb, adverb, adjective, pronoun, or noun, but a word of its own category. Jonathan once sent Bill a study he had found showing that swearing in the workplace enhances morale. Bill's uncharacteristically understated response: "A good one for me!"*

But as Pat Gallagher put it in his eulogy, "Somehow when Bill did it, it didn't seem like swearing." He continued, "We'll see now what God thinks. Bill's been up there in heaven for a week now . . . is it possible for the Lord to take his own name in vain?" Pat tells us that when, shortly before his passing, Bill asked Pat to deliver the eulogy at his service, he did so with an admonishment: "Don't fuck it up!"

We're not sure Bill would have liked the idea of this book very much. He preferred operating behind the scenes, shunned the spotlight when it sought him out, and rejected several inquiries from prospective book authors and agents. But toward the end of his life we believe he had started to come around to the idea. He wouldn't have cared for a biography, but he might have thought that a book that would codify his approach to business coaching and might possibly be helpful in carrying his legacy of success at Apple, Intuit, Google, and the like to other companies—now that might not be such a bad idea after all. We imagine him up there in heaven, leaning back, nodding, and getting used to the idea. Then he leans forward with a big grin on his face and tells us, in his raspy voice, "Don't fuck it up!"

We'll do our best, Coach.

---

* There are numerous studies that report favorable effects of profanity in the workplace: it's good for, among other things, stress relief, honesty, integrity, and creativity. But before you go cussing up a blue streak, you should also know that other studies show that purveyors of profanity are generally judged to be less trustworthy and not as intelligent. Plus, your mom still disapproves.

# CHAPTER 2

# Your Title Makes You a Manager. Your People Make You a Leader.

In July 2001, Google was on the verge of its third birthday and had recently launched the AdWords advertising product, which would soon propel it into the stratosphere. The company had several hundred employees, including many software engineers working under Wayne Rosing, a former Apple and Sun executive who had joined the company six months earlier. Wayne wasn't happy with the performance of his current set of managers. They were strong engineers, but not great managers. So he discussed his concerns with Larry and Sergey, and they came up with a somewhat radical idea that they brought to Eric. They would get rid of all the managers in the engineering organization. Wayne and Eric decided to call it a "disorg": all those software engineers, reporting directly to Wayne.

Larry and Sergey loved the idea. Neither of them had ever worked in a formal business before, and both liked the less structured environment of a university, where students come together for projects, often under the auspices of an advisor, and none are "managed." Coming from the academic world, they had always been skeptical of the role of a manager. Why do you need a manager? Why not just let these supertalented engineers work on projects, and when the project is done, or their work on the project is done, they can go pick another project? If company execs needed to know how a particular project was going, why talk to a manager who may not be actually doing the work? Why not just go talk to the engineer? Never mind that the first manager was probably created within minutes of the first company.* This was Google, where convention went to die.

And so started Google's experiment of running a fast-moving product development team without managers. This was right around the time that Bill started working with the company. Larry and Sergey were just getting used to working alongside Eric, and now they had yet another newcomer hanging around. Bill took his time, getting to know Eric, Larry, Sergey, and other members of the executive team mostly by

---

* If not before the first company! As Peter Drucker astutely pointed out, the greatest manager of all time was probably "the fellow who managed the building of the first pyramid in Egypt some 4,500 years ago."

dropping by in the evenings, when things were more relaxed. He spent the time talking to people about what they were doing and their vision for the company, getting to know the company and the culture.

During one of these conversations Bill mentioned to Larry that "we have to get some managers in here." Larry was nonplussed. After all, he had just gotten rid of all the managers, and he was quite happy with that. Why does a company of several hundred employees, shipping a product that would eventually generate billions in revenue, need managers? Weren't we doing better without them? This went on for a while, the argument going back and forth, both men firm in their convictions. Finally Bill took a page from Larry's book and suggested that they just go talk to the engineers. He, Larry, and Sergey wandered down the hall until they found a couple of software engineers working. Bill asked one of them if he wanted a manager.

Yes, came the response.

Why?

"I want someone I can learn from, and someone to break ties."

They chatted with several software engineers that night, and most of the responses were similar. These engineers *liked* being managed, as long as their manager was someone from whom they could learn something, and someone who helped make decisions. Bill was right! Although it took a while to convince the founders of this: Google engineering continued in "disorg" mode for more than a year. We finally called it quits and brought back people managers near the end of 2002.

In fact, academic research finds merit in both approaches. A 1991 study finds that when a company is in the implementation stage of an innovation (such as when Google was developing its search engine and AdWords), they need managers to help coordinate resources and resolve conflicts. However, a 2005 study finds that creativity flourishes in environments, such as Broadway shows, that are more network-oriented than hierarchical. So there's always tension between creativity and operational efficiency.[1]

To Bill, being an executive of a successful company is all about management, about creating operational excellence. As a manager and CEO, Bill was very good at making sure his teams delivered. He brought people together and created a strong team culture, but never lost sight of the fact that results mattered, and that they were a direct result of good management. "You have to think about how you're going to run a meeting," he told a group of Googlers in a management seminar. "How you're going to run an operations review. You've got to be able to look at someone in a one-on-one and know how to help them course correct. People who are successful run their companies well. They have good processes, they make sure their people are accountable, they know how to hire great people, how to evaluate them and give them feedback, and they pay them well."

Silicon Valley people can get off track, chasing other goals beyond running a good operation. Bill was very good at making sure that it's a results-oriented game. We're going to come together to have a team culture, but it's to achieve results.

Research backs Bill up on this point. A comprehensive 2017 study on manufacturing plants across the United States found that the ones that adopted performance-oriented management techniques, such as monitoring, targeting, and incentives, performed much better than other plants.[2] Good management practices were as important as R&D and IT investments and worker skill level. Good management matters in creative endeavors as well. A 2012 study showed that in the video game industry, strong middle management accounted for 22 percent of the variance in revenue, while game creative design accounted for only 7 percent.[3]

Bill felt that leadership was something that evolved as a result of management excellence. "How do you bring people around and help them flourish in your environment? It's not by being a dictator. It's not by telling them what the hell to do. It's making sure that they feel valued by being in the room with you. Listen. Pay attention. This is what great managers do."

Harvard Business School professor Linda Hill, who studies management and first-time managers in particular, agrees that being a dictator doesn't work. She wrote in 2007, "New managers soon learn . . . that when direct reports are told to do something, they don't necessarily respond. In fact, the more talented the subordinate, the less likely she is to simply follow orders." A manager's authority, she concludes, "emerges only as the manager establishes credibility with subordinates, peers, and superiors."[4] (Another study concludes that people don't just chafe against an authoritarian management style, but are also more likely to leave the team altogether!)[5]

Or, as Bill liked to say: "If you're a great manager, your people will make you a leader. They acclaim that, not you." He attributed this mantra to Donna Dubinsky and usually included the not-so-flattering story behind it. Donna worked with Bill at Apple and Claris, the software company that was spun out of Apple. Bill had been a big shot at Apple, VP of sales and marketing, and had been very successful at Kodak. In both companies he had been detail oriented, frequently micromanaging his team members. That worked pretty well, so when he took on the CEO role at Claris, he figured it was his job to tell everyone what to do. Which he did. Late one afternoon Donna dropped by Bill's office and told him that if he was going to tell everyone what to do, they were all going to quit and go back to Apple. No one wanted to work for a dictator. She added a bit more wisdom for the first-time CEO: "Bill, your title makes you a manager; your people make you a leader." *

Bill took that to heart. He once sent a note to a valuable manager who was struggling, counseling him that "you have demanded respect, rather than having it accrue to you. You need to project humility, a selflessness, that projects that you care about the company and about people."

He was concerned that people he worked with would mistake charisma for leadership, which was somewhat surprising coming from a man who worked closely with Steve Jobs—the poster child for a charismatic business leader—for nearly three decades. But Bill believed that Jobs wasn't a great leader during his first stint at Apple, which ended when

---

* After Donna left Claris, she became CEO of Palm, makers of the PalmPilot. Later she was CEO of Handspring and lead trustee for Yale University, and she is currently the CEO of Numenta, a machine intelligence company.

John Sculley and the board removed him from the company in 1985. When Jobs returned to Apple as CEO in 1997, after Apple had purchased his company NeXT, Bill saw that Steve had changed. "He had always been charismatic, passionate, and brilliant. But when he returned, I watched him become a great manager. He was detailed in everything. Product of course, but also in the way he ran the finance organization, the sales organization, what he did with operations and logistics. I learned from that. Steve couldn't be a good leader until he became a good manager."

So when we met Bill in our weekly coaching sessions, what we discussed first and foremost was management: operations and tactics. Bill rarely weighed in on strategic issues, and if he did, it was usually to make sure that there was a strong operating plan to accompany the strategy. What were the current crises? How quickly were we going to manage our way out of them? How was hiring going? How were we developing our teams? How were our staff meetings going? Were we getting input from everyone? What was being said, what wasn't being said? He cared that the company was well run, and that we were improving as managers.

## IT'S THE PEOPLE

In August 2008, the website Gawker published an article titled "The 10 Most Terrible Tyrants of Tech."[6] "Here's to the screaming ones," the article started, in a parody of the 1997 Richard Dreyfuss–narrated "Think Different" Apple TV ad. "The chair-throwers. The death-threat makers. The imperious gazers. The ones who see things differently—and will stare you down until you do, too. They're not fond of rules, especially those outlined by the human resources department on 'treating your employees with respect.'"

The article went on to list the most notorious of the tech industry's villains: Steve Jobs, Steve Ballmer, Bill Gates, Marc Benioff, and there, second to last, the only Google representative on the list, our own Jonathan Rosenberg. Jonathan was ebullient. He was on a top-ten list featuring the biggest stars of the industry, a hard-ass hall of fame if there ever was one! A few days later, when he walked into his 1:1 with Bill, a printed copy of the article lay on the conference table. Jonathan grinned.

Bill did not. "Jonathan, this is *not* something to be proud of!" Jonathan mumbled some form of response, which Bill cut off with a stream of expletives, concluding with a dagger to Jonathan's weak defense. "What if I were to send this to your mother? What would she think?" They both agreed that Rina Rosenberg would not be happy to see her son on that list.

This is when Bill first shared with Jonathan his "it's the people" manifesto. Bill had developed this while he was at Intuit and often repeated it practically verbatim to the two of us and other coachees.

# IT'S THE PEOPLE

People are the foundation of any company's success. The primary job of each manager is to help people be more effective in their job and to grow and develop. We have great people who want to do well, are capable of doing great things, and come to work fired up to do them. Great people flourish in an environment that liberates and amplifies that energy. Managers create this environment through support, respect, and trust.

Support means giving people the tools, information, training, and coaching they need to succeed. It means continuous effort to develop people's skills. Great managers help people excel and grow.

Respect means understanding people's unique career goals and being sensitive to their life choices. It means helping people achieve these career goals in a way that's consistent with the needs of the company.

Trust means freeing people to do their jobs and to make decisions. It means knowing people want to do well and believing that they will.

---

Numerous academic studies, and constant executive platitudes, show that a company's people should be treated as an asset. But executives often overlook a company's management culture when they are looking for ways to improve performance. This is a mistake: a 1999 article notes that firms that improve their management practices by one standard deviation above the mean can raise their market value by $18,000 per employee.[7] And a Google internal study in 2008 (one that Bill loved) proved that teams with managers who regularly practiced a set of eight behaviors had lower turnover and higher satisfaction and performance. Topping the list of behaviors: "is a good coach."[*]

*It's the people* applies in other arenas as well. For example, Peter Pilling, the athletic director at Columbia, worked with Bill to shift the mission and values of his department. In Peter's case, "it's the people" became "it's the student athletes." Now, when Peter and his team think about a decision, their first consideration is the student athletes. How will that decision affect them, is it consistent with the department's mission to "maximize the opportunities for our student athletes to reach their highest levels of achievement"? Do the student athletes know how much the administrators and coaches care about them? They take a holistic approach to their student athletes, trying to support them in all aspects of their lives, not just the athletic portion. Peter holds quarterly meetings with all of his head coaches, so they can have an open discussion—full candor expected—about their athletes. All of this is a direct result of Bill's principles.

When Brad Smith took over as CEO of Intuit, Bill told him that he would go to bed every night thinking about those eight thousand souls who work for him. What are they thinking and feeling? How can I make them the best they can be?

---

[*] You can read more about Google's "Project Oxygen" study in a December 2013 *Harvard Business Review* article by David Garvin, "How Google Sold Its Engineers on Management."

Ronnie Lott says, when talking about two coaches he worked closely with, Bill Walsh and Bill Campbell: "Great coaches lie awake at night thinking about how to make you better. They relish creating an environment where you get more out of yourself. Coaches are like great artists getting the stroke exactly right on a painting. They are painting relationships. Most people don't spend a lot of time thinking about how they are going to make someone else better. But that's what coaches do. It's what Bill Campbell did, he just did it on a different field."*

"What keeps you up at night?" is a traditional question asked of executives. For Bill the answer was always the same: the well-being and success of his people.

---

## IT'S THE PEOPLE

### THE TOP PRIORITY OF ANY MANAGER IS THE WELL-BEING AND SUCCESS OF HER PEOPLE.

---

* Bill Walsh was the head coach of the San Francisco 49ers for ten years, from 1979 through 1988. His teams won three Super Bowls.

## START WITH TRIP REPORTS

For more than a decade, Eric held his weekly staff meetings on Mondays at 1 p.m. In many ways, these meetings were pretty much like any other staff meeting you might have been to. There was an agenda, check-ins with everyone around the table, people surreptitiously checking email and texts . . . all the usual stuff. Eric did one thing different from the norm, though: when everyone had come into the room and gotten settled, he'd start by asking what people did for the weekend, or, if they had just come back from a trip, he'd ask for an informal trip report. This was a staff that included Larry Page and Sergey Brin, so often the weekend report included kiteboarding tales or updates from the world of extreme fitness, but it also could skew toward the more mundane: Jonathan's daughter's latest soccer achievements, or engineering lead Alan Eustace's score on the golf course.* Sometimes, if he had just returned from a business trip, Eric offered his own report, putting a Google map on the screen with pins dropped on the cities where he'd visited. He'd go city by city, talking about his trip and the interesting things he'd observed.

While this conversation seemed impromptu and informal at first glance, it was a part of a communications approach that Bill had developed over the years and improved in col-

---

* Perhaps some of Larry's and Sergey's adventurous spirit rubbed off on Alan. In October 2014, while on sabbatical from Google, he set the world record for highest-altitude "free-fall" jump when he leapt from a balloon 135,899 feet above the earth's surface. Fourteen minutes later he landed safely, after reaching speeds of 822 mph, successfully completing what Jonathan likes to call "Alan's failure to commit suicide."

laboration with Eric. The objectives were twofold. First, for team members to get to know each other as people, with families and interesting lives outside of work. And second, to get everyone involved in the meeting from the outset in a fun way, as Googlers and human beings, and not just as experts and owners of their particular roles. Bill and Eric understood that there's a direct correlation between fun work environments and higher performance, with conversation about family and fun (what academics might call "socioemotional communication") being an easy way to achieve the former.

Later in the meeting, when business decisions were being discussed, Eric wanted everyone to weigh in, regardless of whether the issue touched on their functional area or not. The simple communications practice—getting people to share stories, to be personal with each other—was in fact a tactic to ensure better decision making and camaraderie.

"At first I thought it was really weird," Dick Costolo says of the trip report practice, which he also learned from Bill. "But when I started doing it and seeing it in practice, wow, it really makes a difference. The whole dynamic of the meeting changes, you get more empathy, a better mood." Dick tells the story of how he attended the staff meeting of a CEO he was mentoring, and the meeting started with hot topics and issues—no social talk whatsoever. "It really hit me in the face how jarring that was. I couldn't tell how well the team worked together and connected."

Marissa Mayer developed a variation of the trip report practice when she was CEO of Yahoo. Rather than trip reports, her staff meetings started with thank-yous. "My staff called it the family prayer. You have to thank another team for something that happened last week. You can't thank yourself, and you can't repeat what someone else said. This ends up being a nice way to recap the entire week."

Bill believed that communications were critical to a company's success. He frequently coached us to make sure that others in the company understood what we understood. Even when you have clearly communicated something, it may take a few times to sink in. Repetition doesn't spoil the prayer. In fact, a 2002 study from Southern Methodist University shows that knowing what to share and communicate and with whom is an important part of a manager's job. Done right, this "knowledge commonality" helps the team perform better and is well worth the time it requires.[8]

Bill had us pay close attention to running meetings well; "get the 1:1 right" and "get the staff meeting right" are tops on the list of his most important management principles. He felt that these meetings are the most important tools available to executives in running the company, and that each one should be approached thoughtfully.

Staff meetings should be a forum for the most important issues and opportunities, more so than 1:1s. "Use meetings to get everyone on the same page, get to the right debate, and make decisions." Most important issues cut across functions, but, more important, bringing them to the table in team meetings lets people understand what is going on in the other teams, and discussing them as a group helps develop understanding and build cross-functional strength. This applies even to some issues that perhaps might be solved in 1:1s, because they give the team practice in tackling challenges together. GO founder Jerry Kaplan recalls, in his book *Startup*, a time when he wanted to discuss GO's growing competition with Microsoft in his 1:1 with Bill. This was a critical topic, requiring detailed discussion of confidential and potentially controversial issues, so a one-on-one between the founder and the CEO seemed like the best forum for it. But Bill said no. He wanted to discuss and decide the issue as a team.[9]

Research confirms that team meetings are a terrific opportunity to engage people, with one 2013 study concluding that the relevance of the meeting, giving everyone a voice, and managing the clock well are key factors to achieving that engagement.[10] This doesn't always happen; another study, from 2015, notes that more than 50 percent of study participants do not think that their meetings are an effective use of their time. This study covered all meetings, not just staff meetings, but still, it demonstrates that being thoughtful about preparing for staff meetings is an important management practice.[11]

---

## START WITH TRIP REPORTS

TO BUILD RAPPORT AND BETTER
RELATIONSHIPS AMONG TEAM
MEMBERS, START TEAM MEETINGS
WITH TRIP REPORTS, OR OTHER
TYPES OF MORE PERSONAL, NON-
BUSINESS TOPICS.

---

# FIVE WORDS ON A WHITEBOARD

Our one-on-one meetings with Bill were always held at his nondescript office off California Avenue, Palo Alto's quieter commercial district a mile or so south of the glitzier University Avenue. This felt like a waste of time at first—why couldn't he come to Google?—but we quickly realized it was the right location. After all, when you go see your therapist, you *go see* your therapist. When making the pilgrimage to Bill, you'd enter through an unmarked door, go up the stairs to the second floor, down a hallway, give Debbie Brookfield, his longtime assistant, a hug, then go into the conference room to wait for him. For Eric's meetings, there were always five words written on the whiteboard, indicating the topics to discuss that day. The words might be about a person, a product, an operational issue, or an upcoming meeting. That's how they organized their talk.

When we were working on this book and Eric talked about his meetings with Bill, Jonathan had to intervene. That was not how Bill started 1:1s, Jonathan reminded Eric. While Bill did have his top-five list of things to discuss, he didn't write them on the whiteboard for all to see. Rather, he would hold them back, like a poker player holding his cards close to the vest. After talking about family and other nonwork stuff, Bill would ask Jonathan what *his* top five items were. Jonathan came to realize that this approach was Bill's way of seeing how Jonathan was prioritizing his time and effort. If Bill led off with *his* list, Jonathan simply could have agreed with it. The discussion of the list was in itself a form of coaching (apparently one that Eric never needed).

In teaching his management seminar at Google, Bill advocated that each person should put his or her list on the board—a simultaneous reveal. That way everyone could see where there was overlap and make sure to cover those topics. He felt that the process of merging the two agendas could serve as a lesson in prioritization.

Regardless of whose five topics go on the whiteboard first, what's important is that each side has a set of topics to cover and is ready to cover them. Bill took great care in preparing for one-on-one meetings. Remember, he believed the most important thing a manager does is to help people be more effective and to grow and develop, and the 1:1 is the best opportunity to accomplish that. Once he became a full-time coach, he varied his approach to suit the person he was coaching. But as a CEO he developed a standard format, which is what he always taught others. He always started with the "small talk," but in Bill's case, the talk wasn't really that small. Oftentimes, small talk in a work environment is cursory: a quick "how are the kids?" or chatter about the morning commute before moving on to the business stuff. Conversations with Bill were more meaningful and layered; you sometimes got the feeling that the conversation about life was more the point of the meeting than the business topics. In fact, while his interest in people's lives was quite sincere, it had a powerful benefit: a 2010 study concludes that having these sort of "substantive" conversations, as opposed to truly small talk, makes people happier.[12]

From the (not so) small talk, Bill moved to performance: What are you working on? How is it going? How could he help? Then, we would always get to peer relationships, which

Bill thought were more important than relationships with your manager and other higher-ups.

One day, Jonathan spent part of his 1:1 with Bill talking about how he wasn't getting any feedback from the founders on his work. What do they want? he wondered. Bill's response was that Jonathan should not worry about top-down feedback; rather, he should pay attention to input from his peers. What do your teammates think of you? That's what's important! They proceeded to talk about Jonathan's peers, how they generally appreciated the work he was doing, and what he could do better.

From peer relationships, Bill would move on to teams. He always wanted to know, were we setting a clear direction for them, and constantly reinforcing it? Did we understand what they were doing? If they were off on something, we would discuss how we could course correct them and get them back on track. "Think that everyone who works for you is like your kids," Bill once said. "Help them course correct, make them better."

Then he'd want to talk about innovation. Were we making space for it on our teams? How were we balancing the inherent tension between innovation and execution? Either alone wasn't good; striking that balance was critical.

Besides having a detailed communications approach, Bill had strong opinions about being good at communicating. He was mostly old-school about it, preferring face-to-face conversations, or a phone call if that wasn't possible. ("You shouldn't wait four weeks to schedule a meeting," he said. "Just get on the phone.") In his CEO days at GO, if you got an email from Bill it was a big deal. Later, when he was coach to people all over the valley, he spent evenings returning the calls of people who had left messages throughout the day. When you left Bill a voice mail, you always got a call back.

He was also great at email. The tendency today is to have cascading emails, a senior person sending something to her staff, who write their own version to their people, and so on. Bill always counseled us to have one email, straight from the senior person, and over the years he practically perfected the art of writing those messages. In researching this book we reread all of the emails we got from Bill over the years and were constantly impressed by just how well written they all were: concise, clear, and compassionate. (When Jonathan's father passed away, Bill wrote, "I am so sorry that I didn't get to know him. He would be very proud of his loving son . . .")

He expected similar quality from everyone around him. Nirav Tolia, the cofounder and CEO of Nextdoor, a social networking site and app for neighborhoods, first met Bill in the summer of 2000, when Nirav was leading a hot dot-com called Epinions. Bill Gurley connected the two of them, and during their first meeting Nirav got a lesson in Bill's approach to communications. "I had a deck prepared for him, and I always put quotes in my decks, stuff from Churchill or similar. So I go through the deck and he let me be the peacock for a while. Finally he stops me. 'Why do you have all those quotes in there?' he wanted to know. 'You haven't told me anything about Epinions.'" He pushed Nirav to scrap the quotes altogether. Just talk about what's going on and what needs to be done.

"Back then, I was ninety percent style, ten percent substance," Nirav remembers. "Bill was one hundred percent substance."

---

## 5 WORDS ON A WHITEBOARD

HAVE A STRUCTURE FOR 1:1s, AND
TAKE THE TIME TO PREPARE FOR
THEM, AS THEY ARE THE BEST
WAY TO HELP PEOPLE BE MORE
EFFECTIVE AND TO GROW.

---

# BILL'S FRAMEWORK
# FOR 1:1s AND REVIEWS

## PERFORMANCE ON JOB REQUIREMENTS

- Could be sales figures
- Could be product delivery or product milestones
- Could be customer feedback or product quality
- Could be budget numbers

## RELATIONSHIP WITH PEER GROUPS
### (This is critical for company integration and cohesiveness)

- Product and Engineering
- Marketing and Product
- Sales and Engineering

## MANAGEMENT/LEADERSHIP

- Are you guiding/coaching your people?
- Are you weeding out the bad ones?
- Are you working hard at hiring?
- Are you able to get your people to do heroic things?

## INNOVATION (BEST PRACTICES)

- Are you constantly moving ahead . . . thinking about how to continually get better?
- Are you constantly evaluating new technologies, new products, new practices?
- Do you measure yourself against the best in the industry/world?

# THE THRONE BEHIND
# THE ROUND TABLE

At one point late in Eric's tenure as CEO of Google, he encountered something familiar to many executives: a turf war.
One of his managers wanted his team to develop a mobile
app for his product's users, but another manager thought that
*his* team should be the one developing the app. The argument
went on for weeks and was progressing from affable to acri-
monious. When his team was confronted with a challenging
decision, Eric liked to use a management technique he called
the "rule of two." He would get the two people most closely
involved in the decision to gather more information and work
together on the best solution, and usually they would come
back a week or two later having decided together on the best
course of action. The team almost always agreed with their
recommendation, because it was usually quite obvious that
it was the best idea. The rule of two not only generates the
best solution in most cases, it also promotes collegiality. It
empowers the two people who are working on the issue to
figure out ways to solve the problem, a fundamental principle
of successful mediation.[13] And it forms a habit of working
together to resolve conflict that pays off with better camaraderie and decision making for years afterward.*[14]

This time around, it wasn't happening. The two executives were dug in. When Eric asked Bill for advice, he replied,

---

* Research on conflict resolution proves that having a standard process
for managing conflict, whether it's the rule of two or another approach,
makes everyone happier and more effective.

"You say, all right, either you two break that tie, or I will."
Eric took Bill's advice, giving the two managers another week
to come to an agreement. They failed, so Eric stepped in and
made the decision.

Bill believed that one of a manager's main jobs is to facil-
itate decisions, and he had a particular framework for doing
so. He didn't encourage democracy. (Before he arrived at Intuit, they took votes in meetings. Bill stopped that practice.)
Rather, he favored an approach not unlike that used in improv comedy. In improv, the entire cast is at risk and needs to
work together to continue a conversation, to put off the final-
ity of a scene until the last possible moment. Bill encouraged
ensembles and always strived for a politics-free environment.
A place where the top manager makes all decisions leads to
just the opposite, because people will spend their time trying
to convince the manager that their idea is the best. In that
scenario, it's not about the best idea carrying the day, it's
about who does the best job of lobbying the top dog. In other
words, politics.

Bill hated that. He believed in striving for the best idea,
not consensus ("I hate consensus!" he would growl), intuitively understanding what numerous academic studies have
shown: that the goal of consensus leads to "groupthink" and
inferior decisions.[15] The way to get the best idea, he believed,
was to get all of the opinions and ideas out in the open, on
the table for the group to discuss. Air the problem honestly,
and make sure people have the opportunity to provide their
authentic opinions, especially if they are dissenting. If the
problem or decision at hand is more functional in nature (for
example, primarily a marketing or finance decision), then the

discussion should be led by the person with that functional expertise. When it is a broader decision cutting across multiple functional areas, then the team leader owns the discussion. Regardless, it should involve everyone's point of view.

To get those ideas on the table, Bill would often sit down with individuals before the meeting to find out what they were thinking. This enabled Bill to understand the different perspectives, but more important, it gave members of his team the chance to come into the room prepared to talk about their point of view. Discussing it with Bill helped gather their thoughts and ideas before the broader discussion. Maybe they would all be aligned by the time they got there, maybe not, but they had already thought through, and talked through, their own perspective and were ready to present it.

As people present and argue ideas, things may become heated. That's to be expected and is fine. As Emil Michael, a Bill coachee and former CBO of Uber, says, "When a leader can get people past being passive-aggressive, then heated but honest arguments can happen." If your team is working well and thinking company-first rather than me-first, then after the fireworks subside the best idea will likely emerge. How the leader frames this discussion matters: a 2016 study shows that when it is called a debate rather than a disagreement, participants are more likely to share information. They perceive that other participants are more receptive to dissenting opinions.[16]

The ensemble approach can be especially hard to implement when the manager in charge of the decision already knows what to do (or thinks she does). Marissa Mayer admits to having had this problem when she was at Google. Then one day Bill gave her a new rule: when she was discussing a decision with her team, she always had to be the last person to speak. You may know the answer and you may be right, he said, but when you just blurt it out, you have robbed the team of the chance to come together. Getting to the right answer is important, but having the *whole team* get there is just as important. So Marissa sat, uncharacteristically quiet, while her team debated issues. She didn't like it, but it worked. She gained new respect for her team and their ability to handle problems.

When the best idea doesn't emerge, it's time for the manager to force the decision or make it herself. "A manager's job is to break ties and make their people better," Bill said. "We're going to do it this way. Cut the shit. Done." Bill learned this the hard way: in his days as an exec at Apple he had experienced the exact opposite, a place where decisions festered and the business suffered. "Apple went to its knees, you know, on those things. You had one division doing this, and another division doing that, and somebody else wanted to do this. People would come to my office and ask me to make the call, but I was the sales and marketing guy, I couldn't break ties between different product groups, between the Apple II group and the Mac group. It was ugly, and nothing got done. That sat with me."

Failure to make a decision can be as damaging as a wrong decision. There's indecision in business all the time, because there's no perfect answer. Do something, even if it's wrong, Bill counseled. Having a well-run process to get to a decision is just as important as the decision itself, because it gives the team confidence and keeps everyone moving. Bruce Chizen, the former CEO of Adobe who worked with Bill at Claris, calls this "making decisions with integrity," which means following a good process and always prioritizing what is the right thing for the business rather than any individual. Make the best decision you can, then move on.

Then, when you make the call, commit to it, and expect that everyone else do so as well. Dan Rosensweig, the CEO of Chegg, a digital learning platform company, once had a situation where he and his CFO had agreed on an important financial move, only to have the CFO try to back out because of a minor issue. Dan called Bill and asked, what should I do?

Bill told Dan about a similar situation he had once faced as CEO. Bill and his management team had decided on a particular strategy, but when Bill presented the strategy at the board meeting, his CFO, who had been on board with the plan, proclaimed that he didn't agree with Bill. After the meeting, Bill asked the CFO to not come back. Even if he didn't agree with the decision, he needed to commit to it. If he couldn't, then he was no longer a member of the team.

This is consistent with the King Arthur round-table model of decision making that Bill described to Brad Smith when Brad became CEO of Intuit. (As Brad tells us this story, he points out the model of the legendary table, with a full complement of seated knights, that sits in the corner of his office.) If you have the right conversation, Bill counseled, then eight out of ten times people will reach the best conclusion on their own. But the other two times you need to make the hard decision and expect that everyone will rally around it.

There isn't a head of that table, but there is a throne behind it.

---

## THE THRONE BEHIND THE ROUND TABLE

### THE MANAGER'S JOB IS TO RUN A DECISION-MAKING PROCESS THAT ENSURES ALL PERSPECTIVES GET HEARD AND CONSIDERED, AND, IF NECESSARY, TO BREAK TIES AND MAKE THE DECISION.

---

# LEAD BASED ON FIRST PRINCIPLES

So how do you make that hard decision? When you are a manager trying to move your team toward making a decision, the room will be rife with opinions. Bill always counseled us to try to cut through those opinions and get to the heart of the matter. In any situation there are certain immutable truths upon which everyone can agree. These are the "first principles," a popular phrase and concept around Silicon Valley. Every company and every situation has its set of them. You can argue opinions, but you generally can't argue principles, since everyone has already agreed upon them. As Bill would point out, it's the leader's job, when faced with a tough decision, to describe and remind everyone of those first principles. As a result, the decision often becomes much easier to make.

Mike McCue was introduced to Bill not long after Mike had raised $250 million for his startup, Tellme Networks, in the 1999 heyday of the dot-com boom. Bill sat in on Tellme's board meetings and some of Mike's staff meetings, and counseled Mike on every important strategic decision he made, both at Tellme and Mike's subsequent company, Flipboard. And since there were lots of strategic decisions to be made, Mike had plenty of opportunities to put into practice Bill's recommendations to decide based on first principles. There was the time AT&T offered to pay tens of millions of dollars to license Tellme's software. Tellme made the first cloud-based speech recognition platform for large businesses and provided the service that answered the phones when you called companies like FedEx, Fidelity, and American Airlines. The problem with the AT&T offer was that they wanted to create a competitive product to Tellme's; in fact, the offer was contingent upon Tellme getting out of the cloud speech recognition business altogether. Oh, and if the deal didn't happen, AT&T, who was at the time Tellme's largest customer, would pull all of its business.

The deal had the potential to be lucrative and Tellme needed the money, so some members of the team were arguing to take it. They honestly thought it was the best decision to make. Mike disagreed, but he knew he wouldn't be successful if he just pushed the team to turn it down. He might win the decision, but he would lose the team.

"They were all really smart people," Mike says. "They had all graduated from great colleges and were great debaters, so there were a lot of opinions. I never went to college, there was no way I was going to win an argument with that group."

(Mike started working right out of high school to help his family after his father died when he was eighteen.) Furthermore, Mike had demoted himself to COO by then, bringing in former Cincinnati Bell executive John LaMacchia as CEO, and John was in favor of taking the AT&T deal.*

So Mike gave Bill a call, then took a walk along the railroad tracks that ran right outside of Tellme's offices. He thought about the first principles involved in the decision. First: the company had a solid business model that was working. Was it smart to take on a new model–software licensing? Second: they had a good product that was, objectively, the best on the market and ahead of its time. Did they think AT&T could make a better product? Probably not. Mike convened the team and laid out these principles. Everyone agreed that they were correct, since they had been foundational for the company for a long time. The decision practically made itself. The meeting concluded in less than an hour, and the deal was off.†

Mike applied the same approach when he was negotiating the sale of Tellme to Microsoft in 2007. He was working directly with Steve Ballmer, the CEO of Microsoft at the time, and at one point the deal was on the verge of collapse because another company came in with an unsolicited offer that was higher than Microsoft's. Mike talked to Bill, thought through

---

* John came in as Tellme's CEO in 2001. He left the company and Mike resumed the CEO role at the end of 2004.

† AT&T ended up deprioritizing its effort to build a competitive product and over time quadrupled its business with Tellme. In 2005, AT&T merged with SBC.

the company's first principles again, and realized that Microsoft was the best home for Tellme. He *wanted* to sell the company to Microsoft. He flew to Redmond, Washington, and walked into Ballmer's office. "Are we going to get divorced before we even get married?" Steve asked Mike. No, Mike responded, and explained why selling the company to Microsoft was the right outcome. Plus, the two of them had already agreed to the basic terms, and Mike had every intent of honoring that agreement (another first principle: integrity). So from that point forward, Steve and Mike became partners in getting the deal completed, with a healthy dose of advice on both sides from Bill. Without Bill's advice to rely on first principles, the deal wouldn't have happened.

## LEAD BASED ON FIRST PRINCIPLES

### DEFINE THE "FIRST PRINCIPLES" FOR THE SITUATION, THE IMMUTABLE TRUTHS THAT ARE THE FOUNDATION FOR THE COMPANY OR PRODUCT, AND HELP GUIDE THE DECISION FROM THOSE PRINCIPLES.

## MANAGE THE ABERRANT GENIUS

Perhaps one of the most difficult problems facing managers is what to do with the diva, the person who's a star performer but a pain to work with. We have certainly come across many of these people during our careers in high-tech, and Bill always reminded us that managing these people is one of the bigger challenges of the job. He called them "aberrant geniuses," and said, "You get these quirky guys or women who are going to be great differentiators for you. It is your job to manage that person in a way that doesn't disrupt the company. They have to be able to work with other people. If they can't, you need to let them go. They need to work in an environment where they collaborate with other people."

So how do you do this? Over the years, through lots of trial and error and with a lot of advice from Bill, we learned this particular art. Support them as they continue to perform, and minimize time spent fighting them. Instead, invest that energy in trying as hard as possible to coach them past their aberrant behavior. As long as you can do this successfully, the rewards can be tremendous: more genius, less aberrant. "He has everything that he needs," Bill once wrote Jonathan about one of his problematic team members. "Now that you fully supported him, you should try to get him to behave as a leader. He has all of his space. No more arguments."

In our experience, aberrant geniuses can be enormously valuable and productive. They can build great products and high-performing teams. They have quick insights. They are simply better in many, many ways. And they can have both the ego and the fragility to match their outsized talent and performance. They often put a lot of energy into personal gains at the expense of peer relationships. A me-first attitude sometimes creeps through (or barges in), which can cause resentment in others and affect their performance.

Here is where the art of balance comes in: there is aberrant behavior, and there is *aberrant* behavior. How much do you tolerate, and when is it too much? Where is that elusive boundary? Never put up with people who cross ethical lines: lying, lapses of integrity or ethics, harassing or mistreating colleagues. In a way, these are the easier cases, since the decision is so clear-cut. The harder cases are the ones where the person doesn't cross these lines. How do you determine when the damage a person causes exceeds their considerable contributions? There's no perfect answer to this, but there are a few warning signs. All of these are coachable, but if there's no change, they shouldn't be tolerated.

Does the aberrant genius break team communications? Does he interrupt others, or attack or rebuke them? Does he make people afraid to talk?

Does the aberrant genius suck up too much management time? It's hard to know when an aberrant genius's behavior has become too toxic for the team to bear, but if you are spending hours upon hours controlling the damage, that's a good sign it's gone too far. A lot of that time is usually spent arguing with the person, which is rarely constructive. One time Bill was coaching a Google manager about an aberrant genius on the team, and he summed up the situation neatly. "I don't know why I'm defending him," Bill noted, "except that his brilliance is one of the things that makes us great. How can we capture the good and dismiss the bad? You can't be with him eighteen hours a day!" The eighteen-hours-a-day comment was an overstatement, but not a huge one; the person was requiring an inordinate amount of management damage control. He eventually left the company.*[17]

Does the aberrant genius have her priorities straight? Eccentric behavior can be okay as long as it is in the service (or intended to be in the service) of the good of the company. What can't be tolerated is when the aberrant genius continually puts him- or herself above the team. This often crops up in areas that are adjacent to the core work of the group. The genius will continue to shine in the job, be it sales, product, legal, and so on. But when it comes to factors such as compensation, press, and promotion, this is where the aberrant pops up.

Does the aberrant genius seek too much attention and self-promotion? Bill wasn't a fan of media attention and mistrusted the motivation of people who sought too much of it. Publicity is fine if it's in the service of the company, and indeed, that is part of the CEO's job. But if you are the CEO and someone on your team is consistently seeking coverage, that's a warning sign. Aberrant geniuses may nominally give credit to their teams but still hog the spotlight. This can have a corrosive effect. People may say it's okay, but over time they start to resent that one person seems to get a lot of credit and other, more humble, people, less. Seeking attention is

---

* A 2017 *Harvard Business Review* article on managing narcissists (which many aberrant geniuses may be), by Manfred F. R. Kets de Vries, includes the recommendation to minimize direct confrontation, which is what a lot of that "eighteen hours" consisted of.

one trait of narcissism, and a 2008 study demonstrates that, controlling for other factors, narcissists are more likely to emerge as group leaders.[18] So having a leader who seeks too much attention maybe isn't all that aberrant. But it can still be problematic if the rest of the team comes to suspect that the media star is more interested in the spotlight than the team's success!

## MANAGE THE ABERRANT GENIUS

ABERRANT GENIUSES—HIGH-PERFORMING BUT DIFFICULT TEAM MEMBERS—SHOULD BE TOLERATED AND EVEN PROTECTED, AS LONG AS THEIR BEHAVIOR ISN'T UNETHICAL OR ABUSIVE AND THEIR VALUE OUTWEIGHS THE TOLL THEIR BEHAVIOR TAKES ON MANAGEMENT, COLLEAGUES, AND TEAMS.

## MONEY'S NOT ABOUT MONEY

Bill helped advise us on compensation issues at Google for many years, and he always advocated generosity. He understood something about compensation that many people do not: the money isn't always about the money. For sure, everyone needs to be paid a fair salary that affords them a good lifestyle. For a great many people, the money *is* about the money.

But it's also about something else. Compensation isn't just about the economic value of the money; it's about the emotional value. It's a signaling device for recognition, respect, and status, and it ties people strongly to the goals of the company. Bill knew that everyone is human and needs to be appreciated, including people who are already financially secure. This is why the superstar athlete who is worth tens or hundreds of millions pushes for that next huge contract. It's not for the money; it's for the love.

---

### MONEY'S NOT ABOUT MONEY

COMPENSATING PEOPLE WELL
DEMONSTRATES LOVE AND
RESPECT AND TIES THEM
STRONGLY TO THE GOALS OF
THE COMPANY.

---

## INNOVATION IS WHERE THE CRAZY PEOPLE HAVE STATURE

When Bill joined Kodak from J. Walter Thompson in 1980, he established himself, according to his Kodak colleague Eric Johnson, as a "virus." He came in with a "Bill way of thinking, a fresh perspective," Eric says. "How do we make things better for Kodak, the dealers, and the consumer?"

Although it may be hard for our under-forty readers to comprehend, there was a long stretch of time when Kodak practically owned photography. You bought a Kodak camera (some of you will remember your first Instamatic; we do!), filled it with Kodak film, and when you had shot all the film, you sent it to a Kodak lab to be processed. By 1976, the company sold 90 percent of the film used in the United States and 85 percent of the cameras.[*][19] So when Bill arrived on the scene in Rochester, he entered a world of unquestioned dominance.

At the time, Kodak's biggest competitor was Fuji, a Japanese company that was starting to challenge Kodak's global hegemony in film. Not long after Bill joined the company, Fuji came out with a film that it promoted as having better quality. And it wasn't just marketing hype—the film actually was better. It was faster, so it could take pictures with less light or a faster shutter speed without compromising the quality of the image. Bill and his colleagues in marketing

---

* A year earlier, in 1975, a Kodak engineer, Steve Sasson, invented the world's first digital camera. And thirty-seven years later, in 2012, the company declared bankruptcy, done in by the shift to digital.

were talking about this new competitive issue one day, when Bill suggested something. How about we go over to the research lab and talk to the engineers? Maybe they can come up with something better, too.

This was not how things worked at Kodak. Marketing guys didn't go talk to engineers, especially the engineers in the research lab. But Bill didn't know that, or if he did, he didn't particularly care. So he went over to the building that housed the labs, introduced himself around, and challenged them to come up with something better than Fuji's latest. That challenge helped start the ball rolling on the film that eventually launched as Kodacolor 200, a major product for Kodak and a film that was empirically better than Fuji's. Score one for the marketing guy and his team!

Bill started his business career as an advertising and marketing guy, then added sales to his portfolio after joining Apple. But through his experiences in the tech world, in his stints at Apple, Intuit, Google, and others, Bill came to appreciate the preeminence of technology and product in the business pecking order. "The purpose of a company is to take the vision you have of the product and bring it to life," he said once at a conference. "Then you put all the other components around it—finance, sales, marketing—to get the product out the door and make sure it's successful." This was not the way things were done in Silicon Valley, or most other places, when Bill came to town in the 1980s. The model then was that while a company might be started by a technologist, pretty soon the powers that be would bring in a business guy, with experience in sales, marketing, finance, or operations, to run the place. These executives wouldn't be thinking about the needs of the engineers and weren't focused on product first. Bill was a business guy, but he believed that nothing was more important than an empowered engineer. His constant point: product teams are the heart of the company. They are the ones who create new features and new products.

The ultimate objective of product teams is to create great product market fit. If you have the right product for the right market at the right time, then go full steam ahead. Eddy Cue, an Apple executive who helped create the App Store, recalls that when he first presented the concept of the store to the Apple board, Bill quickly grasped the bigger picture of how important it was. It seemed to some like it was something that was merely nice to have, but Bill realized its immense potential. "Others were asking nuts-and-bolts questions about how it worked," Eddy says, "while Bill's questions were all about how we can move faster." This was a constant theme from Bill and something he preached to us and others: if you have the right product for the right market at the right time, *go as fast as you can.* There are minor things that will go wrong and you have to fix them quickly, but speed is essential.

This means that finance, sales, or marketing shouldn't tell the product teams what to do. Instead, these groups can supply intelligence on what customer problems need solving, and what opportunities they see.*[20] They describe the market part

---

* Innovative product teams should use problem intelligence as only a starting point. In a January–February 2017 article in *Harvard Business Review,* author and consultant Thomas Wedell-Wedellsborg notes that many teams searching for solutions to problems fail to consider if they are solving the right problem. Wedell-Wedellsborg outlines seven practices to "re-frame" problems, which can lead to new and surprising solutions.

of "product market fit." Then they stand by, let the product teams work, and clear the way of things that might slow them down. As Bill often commented, "Why is marketing losing its clout? Because it forgot its first name: product."

Bill liked to tell a story about when he was at Intuit and they started getting into banking products. They hired some product managers with banking experience. One day, Bill was at a meeting with one of those product managers, who presented his engineers with a list of features he wanted them to build. Bill told the poor product manager, if you ever tell an engineer at Intuit which features you want, I'm going to throw you out on the street. You tell them what problem the consumer has. You give them context on who the consumer is. Then let them figure out the features. They will provide you with a far better solution than you'll ever get by telling them what to build.

This does not mean you let engineers run off, unfettered, doing whatever they please. To the contrary, product teams need to partner with those other teams from the outset, integrated into a cross-functional group that pushes forward with new ideas that solve problems and hatch opportunities. Remember, Bill was the marketing guy who literally walked down the street to work with engineers on a problem. It does mean that the engineers (and other people creating products) have clout, and that they need to be given some freedom. Ron Sugar, an Apple board member and former CEO of Northrop Grumman, says, "Bill helped me understand that in a company like Apple, the degree of independence of creative thinking, of being not so conformist, is a strength. You need to embrace that nonconformist streak."

When Bill was CEO of Intuit, he met with all the engineering directors for lunch every Friday, where they'd spend a couple of hours over pizza talking about what they were doing and what was slowing them down. For a non-techie, Bill did a good job getting into details with the geeks; the execs need to be able to talk to the engineers, even if they aren't engineering execs. And the geeks knew they had the CEO's attention every week. This is how he ensured that they had stature.

---

## INNOVATION IS WHERE THE CRAZY PEOPLE HAVE STATURE

THE PURPOSE OF A COMPANY IS TO BRING A PRODUCT VISION TO LIFE. ALL THE OTHER COMPONENTS ARE IN SERVICE TO PRODUCT.

---

## HEADS HELD HIGH

In business, layoffs and firings are inevitable, perhaps more so in the world of startups and technology. Bill's point of view on this was that letting people go is a failure of management, not one of any of the people who are being let go. So it is important for management to let people leave with their heads held high. Treat them well, with respect. Be generous with severance packages. Send out a note internally celebrating their accomplishments.

Bill would actually practice these scenarios with his coachees. Shishir Mehrotra, whom Bill coached throughout his career, once had to fire one of his engineering leads at a startup where he was working. Before Shishir had the conversation with the person, he and Bill walked through how he was going to conduct the meeting, line by line, even thinking through the practical details of who would sit where in the conference room. Be clear about it early in the conversation, Bill said. Go through your reasoning and provide details. Shishir knew that the move was going to be a surprise to the engineer, for which Bill scolded him. "Bill told me that I had screwed up," Shishir says. "It shouldn't have been a surprise."

As Ben Horowitz notes in his book, *The Hard Thing About Hard Things*, treating the departing people well is important for the morale and well-being of the remaining team. "Many of the people whom you lay off will have closer relationships with the people who stay than you do, so treat them with the appropriate level of respect. Still, the company must move forward, so be careful not to apologize too much." Research confirms this point: laid-off employees care about who's doing the layoffs, and how good an explanation they get. Doing layoffs properly has a positive impact on both the people being laid off and the people who stay on with the company.[21]

Firing people (terminating someone for performance issues) demands a similar level of respect. It has to be done sometimes, and it's tough. Bill would tell us, "When you fire someone, you feel terrible for about a day, then you say to yourself that you should have done it sooner. No one ever succeeds at their third chance." If you've ever had the crappy task of firing someone, and you think back on that experience, you will realize that this is absolutely correct. But again, you must let people leave with their heads held high.

As Bill once told Ben Horowitz about a departing executive: "Ben, you cannot let him keep his job, but you absolutely can let him keep his respect."[22]

---

## HEADS HELD HIGH

IF YOU HAVE TO LET PEOPLE
GO, BE GENEROUS, TREAT THEM
WELL, AND CELEBRATE THEIR
ACCOMPLISHMENTS.

---

## BILL ON BOARDS

Imagine for a moment you are a member of the Apple board of directors. It is the late 2000s, and you have just completed a long day at the company's headquarters in Cupertino, California, reviewing financial information and getting an advance look at the latest in a string of dazzling new products. You are tired but excited; remember, about a decade ago this company was almost bankrupt! You, your fellow board members, and a handful of Apple execs travel to a sushi restaurant called Mitsunobu in nearby Menlo Park to relax and have some fun after a busy day. It's a big enough group that you have to split up into a couple of tables in a private dining room. You have a glass of wine and are enjoying some tasty salmon sashimi while you discuss serious things with the distinguished people at your table.

Suddenly, a burst of laughter from the other table interrupts the placid atmosphere, followed by a shout, then another outburst. Annoyed, you look over just as Bill Campbell throws his napkin across the table at Al Gore, who grabs it off his forehead and throws it right back. Bill continues the story he was telling, as Al and the rest of the table burst out laughing again. It's like a holiday supper where you are sitting with the other adults, while the other table, full of kids, has all the fun. I wish I were sitting with them, you think.

Bill Campbell knew how to have fun. He made every table the kids' table, even at dinners following board meetings, which are usually sedate (aka boring) affairs. Bill was only officially on a few boards (including Apple's), but he participated informally in many others and had plenty of experience managing them as a CEO at Claris, GO, and Intuit. He knew how to occasionally have fun with boards, but he also developed a strong set of guidelines on how CEOs should work with their boards to get the most out of them. A good, effective board can be a tremendous asset to a company, while a weak one just sucks up time. Getting this right matters, and whether or not you are a CEO with the responsibility to manage a board, his approach provides good insights for managing any kind of big meeting of people who are short on time and long on ego.

Bill's perspective on boards starts with this observation: the CEO manages the board and board meetings, not the other way around.*[23] Board meetings fail when the CEO doesn't own and follow her agenda. That agenda should always start with operational updates: the board needs to know how the company is doing. That includes financial and sales reports, product status, and metrics around operational rigor (hiring, communications, marketing, support). If the board has committees, for example to oversee audit and finance or compensation, have those committees meet ahead of time (in person or via phone or video conference) and present updates at the board meeting. The first order of business always needs to be

---

* Who manages whom is often a source of tension on boards. As a 2003 paper from the University of California, Berkeley, says, "The CEO has incentives to 'capture' the board, so as to ensure that he can keep his job and increase the other benefits he derives from being CEO. Directors have incentives to maintain their independence, to monitor the CEO, and to replace the CEO if his performance is poor."

a frank, open, succinct discussion about how the company is performing.

Much of this material can be sent to board members ahead of time, with the idea that they will review it and be up-to-date on most stuff when they come to the meeting. If you throw a full set of financial reports up on a screen in a board meeting, they will want to talk about it forever, and you end up getting bogged down in operational details that probably don't need the board's attention. Send out financial and other operational details ahead of time and expect board members to review them and come with questions.

And when we say expect, we mean *expect*: board members who don't do their homework shouldn't stick around. Dan Rosensweig once had a guy on his board at Chegg who wouldn't read anything ahead of the board meeting and then spent a lot of time at the meeting asking about details that were in his preread. At one board meeting, Dan got angry at him for wasting everyone's time. Afterward, Bill, who was at the meeting, told Dan that he shouldn't lose his cool like that. Send the guy an information packet a week ahead of time and tell him exactly which pages you are going to cover in the meeting and exactly what you expect him to do. So that's what Dan did. And the same thing happened: the guy showed up unprepared and wasted a lot of time asking questions about things he should have known already.

Yeah, I was wrong, Bill told Dan afterward. Fire him.

In our board meetings at Google, Bill always pushed Eric to ensure that the operations review included a thorough set of highlights and lowlights. Here's what we did well and what we're proud of; here's what we didn't do so well. The highlights were always easy to compile; teams love dressing up their best successes and presenting them to the board. But the lowlights, not so much. It can take some prodding to make teams be completely frank about where they are falling short, and indeed, Eric often rejected an initial draft of the board lowlights for not being honest enough. He was dogged in ensuring that the lowlights were authentic, and as a result, the board would see the bad news along with the good.

Creating a robust set of real lowlights might entail giving honest updates on things ranging from revenue growth and product limitations to employee attrition and concerns about the pace of innovation. A 2002 *Harvard Business Review* article notes that a "virtuous cycle of respect, trust, and candor" is one thing that makes "great boards great."[24] And this level of honesty sets a tone of transparency and honesty that reverberates throughout the company. A company that is honest with its board can be honest with itself, too; people learn that not only is it okay to frankly share bad news, it's expected. Determining lowlights is an important task, something to be handled by people running the business, not left to support functions such as finance or communications. At Google, we had product managers handle the task.

But . . . we would *not* include the highlights and lowlights in the packet of information that we sent to board members ahead of the meeting. If you do that, they will spend too much time obsessing about the lowlights and will want to start the meeting there.

Who should be on the board? Smart people with good

business expertise who care deeply about the company and are genuinely interested in helping and supporting the CEO. When Dick Costolo took the role of CEO of Twitter, the board consisted of several venture capitalists, some members of the founding team, and Dick. Bill helped Dick change that and bring in more people with lots of expertise in actually running businesses. You need some other operators to lean on, he told Dick.

He was also quite clear about what a *bad* board member looks like: "Someone who just walks in and wants to be the smartest guy in the room and talks too much."

---

## BILL ON BOARDS

### IT'S THE CEO'S JOB TO MANAGE BOARDS, NOT THE OTHER WAY AROUND.

---

We talk more in subsequent chapters about Bill's role as a coach, at Google and numerous other companies, and about how he made an enormous impact in this unique role. But he also had tremendous acumen as an executive. Remember, this was a guy who went from college football coach to senior executive at a Fortune 500 company in less than five years. He was a superb business executive. And he did it through practicing the points covered in this chapter: operational excellence, putting people first, being decisive, communicating well, knowing how to get the most out of even the most challenging people, focusing on product excellence, and treating people well when they are let go.

# CHAPTER 3

# Build an Envelope of Trust

At one point when Bill Campbell was CEO of Intuit, the company was having a rough quarter and it looked like it might not make its revenue and profit objectives. When the board got together to discuss what to do about it, most of its members were willing to tolerate missing short-term financial targets, as they felt it was more important for the company to invest in the future. Short-term objectives weren't as important as long-term growth, which might be sacrificed if spending was curtailed. Bill disagreed. He wanted to get leaner and make the numbers. That is the culture we want to have around here, he explained. It wasn't so much about hitting those short-term numbers, but about creating a culture where anything less than operational excellence wouldn't be tolerated. He felt it was management's job to deliver results, not just for shareholders but for the team and customers. The board wanted to focus on the long run by investing; Bill knew that he was also investing in the long-term success of the company by instilling strong operational discipline.

This particular moment was shaping up as an unusual disagreement between a forgiving board and a disciplined former football coach turned CEO. As the conversation moved around the room, most of the board members wanted to spend their way through the crisis, to invest in the future. They disagreed with their CEO. Finally, it was John Doerr's turn to weigh in. "You know," he said, "I think we should back the coach." John says that was the moment when he earned Bill Campbell's trust. "The board may have been correct," he says. "But isn't the real right answer to back your CEO?" It almost didn't matter what the debate was about; it was something that Bill felt passionate about, and John decided to bet on Bill. He trusted him.

Perhaps the most important currency in a relationship—friendship, romantic, familial, or professional—is trust. This was certainly true with Bill Campbell. If Bill didn't trust you, you didn't have a relationship with him. But if he did trust you, and vice versa, that trust was the basis for all other aspects of the relationship. Trust is of course important for any relationship, but in most business relationships it takes its place alongside other factors: personal agendas, mutual exchange of value. For Bill, trust was always first and foremost; it was sort of his superpower. He was great at establishing it, and once established, he was great at honoring it. In one of the last times they saw each other, Bill told Alan Eustace,

"You know I would do anything for you." He meant it, because of the trust between them.

Trust is a multifaceted concept, so what do we mean by it? One academic paper defines trust as "the willingness to accept vulnerability based upon positive expectations about another's behavior."[1] That's a bit of an academic mouthful, but it captures the essential point that trust means people feel safe to be vulnerable. When we are referring to Bill and trust, it means a few things.

Trust means you keep your word. If you told Bill you were going to do something, you did it. And the same applied to him; his word was *always* good.

Trust means loyalty. To each other, to your family and friends, and to your team and company. Bill was one of the few Apple executives to fight to keep Steve Jobs when he was let go from the company in 1985. Steve never forgot that expression of loyalty, which later became the basis for their close friendship and working relationship.

Trust means integrity. Bill was always honest, and he expected the same in return. And it means ability, the trust that you actually had the talent, skills, power, and diligence to accomplish what you promised.

Trust means discretion. When Eric was CEO of Google, one of his team members was diagnosed with a serious medical condition (he later fully recovered) but chose not to share it with Eric or the rest of the team. The only person who knew was Bill, who told no one. Eric later found out, and rather than be annoyed that Bill kept the information from him, he was happy to learn that Bill was so trustworthy. Bill could keep a secret, even from Eric, and so could act as a confidant to anyone on the team. This is very valuable to a coach, who always needs to know what's going on, but also needs to be seen by his coachees as someone who honors their privacy.

Perhaps the idea that trust is a cornerstone of business success belongs in the "well duh, Captain Obvious" bucket. But it is missing from many of today's business books, and it never came up as a factor in Google's success when we were researching and writing our previous book, *How Google Works*. So it was somewhat of a surprise to us that when we interviewed the dozens of successful businesspeople Bill had mentored, the word came up again and again. Dean Gilbert, a former executive at Google and @Home, and an accomplished management coach in his own right, notes that "Bill would build an envelope of trust very quickly. It was a natural thing for him, this ability to build rapport, a sense of comfort and protection. It's the cornerstone of any coaching in business." Vinod Khosla, a Sun Microsystems cofounder and head of Khosla Ventures, says that he and Bill "built a great relationship around trust, whether we agreed or disagreed." An important point: trust doesn't mean you always agree; in fact, it makes it easier to disagree with someone. These are just a couple of the numerous quotes we could cite from people who worked with Bill, all of them basically saying the same thing: You could trust Bill. His success stemmed from that.

A slew of academic research bears out what Bill intuitively knew—not just that trust is important, but that it is the *first* thing to create if you want a relationship to be successful. It is the foundation. For example, a highly cited 2000 study from Cornell University discusses the correlation between task conflict (disagreements about decisions) and relationship conflict (emotional friction) in teams. Task conflict is healthy and is important to get to the best decisions, but it is highly correlated with relationship conflict, which leads to poorer decisions and morale. What to do? Build trust *first*, the study concludes. Teams that trust each other will still have disagreements, but when they do, they will be accompanied by less emotional rancor.[2]

Most business people, when they meet, get right to the task at hand. There's stuff to do! This is especially true in technology, technologists not being noted for their high EQs or social skills. In our world, the attitude is often first prove to me how smart you are, then maybe I'll trust you, or at least your intellect. Bill took a different, more patient approach. He started relationships by getting to know the person, beyond their résumé and skill set. Shishir Mehrotra notes that Bill "walked among a set of driven technologists, but he saw the world in a completely different way . . . He saw it as a network of people, learning each other's strengths and weaknesses, and learning to trust each other as a primary mechanism of achieving goals."

Trust is also an important theme among the best sports coaches (and was the subject of Bill's pregame talk to the Stanford football team, when he was made honorary captain for a game in 2012). Red Auerbach, who as a coach and executive led the Boston Celtics to sixteen NBA championships in thirty years (including a remarkable eight straight), had a simple way of expressing the importance of trust: "The players won't con me because I don't con them."[3] He believed that level of trust led to stability and to greater commitment from his players: "When players find themselves in a situation where management has a great deal of integrity and they can depend on my word or anybody else's word in the organization, they feel secure. And if the players feel secure, they don't want to leave here. And if they don't want to leave here, they're going to do everything they can on the court to stay here."

Establishing trust is a key component to building what is now called "psychological safety" in teams. Team psychological safety, according to a 1999 Cornell study, is a "shared belief held by members of a team that the team is safe for interpersonal risk taking . . . a team climate . . . in which people are comfortable being themselves."[4] This is exactly the feeling we experienced when working with Bill; he quickly established a relationship where we could be ourselves, without fear. Not surprisingly, when Google conducted a study to determine the factors behind high-performing teams, psychological safety came out at the top of the list.[*] The common notions that the best teams are made up of people with complementary skill sets or similar personalities were disproven; the best teams are the ones with the most psychological safety. And that starts with trust.

It's hard to disagree with the notion that trust is essential for productive relationships. But in the high-stakes, big-ego world of business executives, it is easier said than done (espe-

---

[*] More details about the study can be found in James Graham, "What Google Learned from Its Quest to Build the Perfect Team," *New York Times*, February 25, 2016.

cially when you remember that our protagonist, Coach Bill, had quite a healthy ego of his own and the opinions and stubbornness to match). How did Bill do it? First, he only coached the coachable. Then, if you passed that test, he listened intently, practiced complete candor, believed that his coachees could achieve remarkable things, and was intensely loyal.

## ONLY COACH THE COACHABLE

On a January day in 2002, Jonathan drove over to the Google office in Mountain View, where he thought he was going to pick up a formal job offer to become head of the growing Google product team. He thought the job was a lock, but once he arrived, he was escorted to a plain conference room where a gruff, older guy greeted him. It was the first time Jonathan met Bill. He couldn't quite remember who Bill was, and did not realize, at least at first, that this guy was the final gateway on the road to employment at the company. No problem, thought Jonathan, I'm a pretty big deal, SVP from a successful tech company, @Home. I got this!

Bill looked at Jonathan for what seemed like minutes, then told him that he had spoken with a few of the principals from @Home: its cofounder Tom Jermoluk; its first CEO, William Randolph Hearst III; and one of its investors, John Doerr, who was also on Google's board. The consensus, Bill reported, was that Jonathan was smart and worked hard. Jonathan's chest puffed a bit.

"But I don't care about any of that," Bill said. "I only have one question: Are you coachable?"

Jonathan instantly, and regrettably, replied: "It depends on the coach."

Wrong answer.

"Smart alecks are *not* coachable," Bill snapped. He stood up to leave, interview over, as it dawned on Jonathan that he had heard Eric Schmidt was getting coaching from someone and, oh my God, this must be the guy. Jonathan switched from smart-aleck mode to groveling mode, backing away from his quip (which wasn't exactly a quip), and asked Bill to continue the conversation. After another moment that felt like minutes, Bill sat back down and talked about how he chose the people he was going to work with based on humility. Leadership is not about you, it's about service to something bigger: the company, the team. Bill believed that good leaders grow over time, that leadership accrues to them from their teams. He thought people who were curious and wanted to learn new things were best suited for this. There was no room in this formula for smart alecks and their hubris.

Bill then asked, "What do you want to get out of a coach?"

This felt like, and indeed was, a change-your-life-forever moment. And Jonathan couldn't think of anything to say. Finally and fortunately, in what football fans might call a Hail Mary play, he remembered a quote from Tom Landry, who coached the NFL's Dallas Cowboys for twenty-nine years, a stint that included twenty straight winning seasons and two Super Bowl titles. "A coach is someone who tells you what you don't want to hear, who has you see what you don't want to see, so you can be who you have always known you could be." That's what I want, Jonathan told Bill.

It worked. Jonathan not only got the job, he got the coach he didn't think he needed, but sorely did.

People who want to get the best out of a coaching relationship need to be coachable. Bill's approach to coaching was rooted in his mind-set that almost all people have value, not based on their title or role but on who they are. His job was to make them better. But only if they were coachable. And, Jonathan's experience notwithstanding, that was based on a lot more than the ability to pull a pithy quote out of the ether (or nether) in a pinch.

The traits of coachability Bill sought were honesty and humility, the willingness to persevere and work hard, and a constant openness to learning. Honesty and humility because a successful coaching relationship requires a high degree of vulnerability, *much* more than is typical in a business relationship. Coaches need to learn how self-aware a coachee is; they need to not only understand the coachee's strengths and weaknesses, but also understand how well the coachee understands his or her own strengths and weaknesses. Where are they honest with themselves, and where are their blind spots? And then it is the coach's job to raise that self-awareness further and to help them see the flaws they don't see for themselves. People don't like to talk about these flaws, which is why honesty and humility are so important. If people can't be honest with themselves and their coach, and if they aren't humble enough to recognize how they aren't perfect, they won't get far in that relationship.

Humility, because Bill believed that leadership is about service to something that is bigger than you: your company, your team. Today the concept of "servant leadership" is in vogue and has been directly linked to stronger company performance.*[5] Bill believed and practiced it well before it became popular. The coachable people are the ones who can see that they are part of something bigger than themselves. You can have a considerable ego and still be part of an even bigger cause. This is one reason Bill threw himself into coaching people at Google. He foresaw that the company had the potential to have a big impact in the world, to indeed be far bigger in every way than any of its individual execs.

The flip side of the honest, humble person is the bullshitter. "Bill couldn't stand BSers," John Hennessy says. He's the former president of Stanford University who worked closely with Bill on several fronts. Bill's opposition to bullshitters wasn't as much about their dishonesty with others as it was about their dishonesty with themselves. To be coachable, you need to be brutally honest, starting with yourself. As Hennessy says, "People who generate a lot of BS aren't coachable. They start to believe what they are saying. They shade the truth to conform to their BS, which makes the BS even more dangerous."

Perhaps this intolerance came from Bill's football days. As Hennessy puts it, "There's no room for BS on the football field!"

---

* A 2012 study demonstrates that tech companies have higher return on assets (ROA) when CEOs are servant leaders and lower ROA when CEOs are narcissists.

## ONLY COACH THE COACHABLE

### THE TRAITS THAT MAKE A PERSON COACHABLE INCLUDE HONESTY AND HUMILITY, THE WILLINGNESS TO PERSEVERE AND WORK HARD, AND A CONSTANT OPENNESS TO LEARNING.

## PRACTICE FREE-FORM LISTENING

In a coaching session with Bill, you could expect that he would listen intently. No checking his phone for texts or email, no glancing at his watch or out the window while his mind wandered. He was always right there. Today it is popular to talk about "being present" or "in the moment." We're pretty sure those words never passed the coach's lips, yet he was one of their great practitioners. Al Gore says he learned from Bill how "important it is to pay careful attention to the person you are dealing with . . . give them your full, undivided attention, really listening carefully. Only then do you go into the issue. There's an order to it."

Alan Eustace called Bill's approach "free-form listening"—academics might call it "active listening," a term first coined in 1957[6]—and in practicing it Bill was following the advice of the great UCLA basketball coach John Wooden, who felt that poor listening was a trait shared by many leaders: "We'd all be a lot wiser if we listened more," Wooden said, "not just hearing the words, but listening and not thinking about what we're going to say."[7]

Bill's listening was usually accompanied by a lot of questions, a Socratic approach. A 2016 *Harvard Business Review* article notes that this approach of asking questions is essential to being a great listener: "People perceive the best listeners to be those who periodically ask questions that promote discovery and insight."[8]

"Bill would never tell me what to do," says Ben Horowitz. "Instead he'd ask more and more questions, to get to what the real issue was." Ben found an important lesson in Bill's technique that he applies today when working with his fund's CEOs. Often, when people ask for advice, all they are really asking for is approval. "CEOs always feel like they need to know the answer," Ben says. "So when they ask me for advice, I'm always getting a prepared question. I never answer those." Instead, like Bill, he asks more questions, trying to understand the multiple facets of a situation. This helps him get past the prepared question (and answer) and discover the heart of an issue.

Listening well helps ensure that all ideas and perspectives get surfaced. Jerry Kaplan tells a story in *Startup*, his book about GO, about how the management team decided to shift the architecture of their computing system from Intel-based processors to RISC-based ones. (*RISC* stands for *Reduced Instruction Set Computer.* Today, most computers are RISC-based, as are most smartphones.)

Bill was the CEO, but as Jerry tells the story, this major strategic decision emerged from a rowdy management meeting where Bill teed up the problem (they were starting to compete with Microsoft, so perhaps they should "go where they aren't") and let his team throw out the best ideas. They argued for a while and were initially incredulous when Mike Homer, who had worked with Bill at Apple (and became a lifelong friend), came up with the idea to shift processors, and Robert Carr, the company's cofounder and head of software, suggested RISC. But it gradually became obvious that the new idea was the best, so that's what they did.[9]

When you listen to people, they feel valued. A 2003 study from Lund University in Sweden finds that "mundane, almost trivial" things like listening and chatting with employees are important aspects of successful leadership, because "people feel more respected, visible and less anonymous, and included in teamwork."[10] And a 2016 paper finds that this form of "respectful inquiry," where the leader asks open questions and listens attentively to the response, is effective because it heightens the "follower's" feelings of competence (feeling challenged and experiencing mastery), relatedness (feeling of belonging), and autonomy (feeling in control and having options). Those three factors are sort of the holy trinity of the self-determination theory of human motivation, originally developed by Edward L. Deci and Richard M. Ryan.[11]

As Salar Kamangar, an early Google executive, puts it, "Bill was uplifting. No matter what we discussed, I felt heard, understood, and supported."*

---

* Among other notable Google accomplishments, Salar helped create Google's flagship advertising product, AdWords, and later led YouTube.

---

## PRACTICE FREE-FORM LISTENING

### LISTEN TO PEOPLE WITH YOUR FULL AND UNDIVIDED ATTENTION— DON'T THINK AHEAD TO WHAT YOU'RE GOING TO SAY NEXT—AND ASK QUESTIONS TO GET TO THE REAL ISSUE.

---

## NO GAP BETWEEN STATEMENTS AND FACT

One day Bill dropped by Dan Rosensweig's office at Chegg. Dan had just given an upbeat presentation at the board meeting. The company, which had been on the verge of going under, was in a much more stable position. Not growing, but at least not failing. Dan and his team were in a celebratory mood.

Bill walked into the office sporting a green eyeshade, the kind accountants used to wear in the early parts of the twentieth century to reduce eye strain. He went around the office space, greeting people at their desks before eventually arriving at Dan's door. Congratulations, he said, you saved the company. You are now the most successful nongrowth CEO in the valley! The accountants may be happy, but that's about it, because that's not what you came here to do, is it? He hugged Dan, then chucked the eyeshade at him. Dan realized in that moment that he had solved only one problem, a big one, but Bill was right. Dan didn't want to just save the company, he wanted to grow it. The truth was a bit of a slap in the face, but it was time to get back to work.

Bill was always 100 percent honest (he told the truth) and candid (he wasn't afraid to offer a harsh opinion). A straight shooter if there ever was one. Google board member and former Amazon executive Ram Shriram: "Bill was always transparent; there was no hidden agenda. There was no gap between his statements and fact. They were always the same." Intuit cofounder Scott Cook: "He really taught me about honesty and authenticity in giving feedback. You can keep someone's respect and loyalty while delivering tough news about their performance."

Bill's candor worked because we always knew it was coming from a place of caring. Former Googler Kim Scott, author of the excellent book *Radical Candor*, says that being a great boss means "saying what you really think in a way that still lets people know you care."[12] In the Dan Rosensweig anecdote, for example, Bill accomplishes this with humor, delivering a tough message (nongrowth CEO) with a funny prop (green eyeshade). You'd have to care to wear that thing!

An important component of providing candid feedback is not to wait. "A coach coaches in the moment," Scott Cook says. "It's more real and more authentic, but so many leaders shy away from that." Many managers wait until performance reviews to provide feedback, which is often too little, too late. Bill's feedback was in the moment (or very close to it), task specific, and always followed by a grin and a hug, all of which helped remove the sting.

He'd also make sure that if the feedback was critical, to deliver it in private. Diane Greene, the head of Google Cloud and former VMware CEO who worked with Bill when they were on the board at Intuit, learned from Bill to never embarrass someone publicly. "When I'm really annoyed or frustrated with what someone is doing," she says, "I step back and force myself to think about what they are doing well and what their value is. You can always find something. If we're in public, I'll praise them on that. I'll give constructive feedback as soon as I can, but only when the person is feeling safe. Once they are feeling safe and supported, then I'll say 'by the way' and provide the feedback. I got this from Bill. He would always do this in a supportive way."

Pat Gallagher was in the front office of the San Francisco Giants for many years before they moved into the beautiful AT&T Park and won three world championships. He was Bill's neighbor and friend, but also a recipient of some of his legendary candor. You're the marketing guy with the worst ballpark in America (the regrettable Candlestick Park, the team's previous home) and a shitty team, Bill told Pat (we assume Pat was in a safe place at the time!). You'd better do everything you can to make the customer experience great! It's all you've got.

Jesse Rogers has a similar story. He became Bill's friend because their kids went to Sacred Heart together, but became his coachee as he was trying to decide if he should leave his job and strike out on his own. The two talked about it a lot, and Jesse decided to make the jump. A few weeks later, as he was getting set up in his new office, he sent Bill the link to the brand-new website of the firm he had cofounded, Altamont Capital. A few minutes later, Jesse's phone rang. He expected some nice words of congratulations, a verbal pat on the back. Instead, "Your website is a piece of shit!" was how Bill said hello. Followed by a couple more minutes of ranting on how the Altamont website was not up to snuff. This was Silicon Valley; you couldn't be a successful startup here and have a shitty website! It was a full minute or two before Jesse could say anything. "Bill's natural state is to be oppositional and challenge you," Jesse says. "The great thing about Bill is that he is aggressive and tenacious in giving negative feedback."*

Bill was candid with the kids, too. Jonathan's daughter, Hannah, grew up wanting to play big-time college soccer, which in the United States means Division I. Bill watched her play, then told her, sure, she could make a Division I college team and might even start at some programs. Or she could go to a Division III school and be a star while getting a great education. Hannah was deflated, but she knew the coach was right. She subsequently graduated with a degree in engineering from Washington University in St. Louis, helped them win an NCAA Division III championship her senior year, and earned a Scholar All-America award.

Of course, being Bill, sometimes that candor could be

---

* Jesse was one of several people to use the present tense when talking about Bill, even though all of our interviews took place after Bill's passing. Many said they still think about Bill and about how he would advise them whenever they are making decisions.

presented in fairly raw language. Mason Randall was a star athlete at Sacred Heart and the quarterback of the eighth-grade flag football team, which Bill coached. One day they were playing archrival Menlo. Mason threw a late interception, which helped contribute to a Sacred Heart loss. He was walking off the field, head low, dejected, when Bill came up beside him. He stuck his forefinger in his cheek, popped it out, and said, "Mason! What's that?"

"It's the sound of my head coming out of my ass?" the eighth grader asked, repeating an oft-heard Bill phrase.

"That's right. Get your head up! We lost this one as a team!"

The interesting thing is—and our experience with Bill bears this out—that his candor, no matter how brutal, made you feel better. This seems counterintuitive; after all, having someone tell you how badly you screwed up should feel pretty crummy. But coming from Bill it didn't; the formula of candor plus caring works well! We trusted that Bill was kicking our butts to help make us better. As Vinod Khosla says, "Lots of people won't actually state their mind. Bill always stated what he was thinking. But he did it in a way that even if people were disappointed, they were charged up about it! That's an unusual talent."

Dave Kinser, Bill's head of operations at Claris, recalls a time that Bill was going to chew out one of Dave's fellow executives. Before the "ball busting," Bill approached Dave, told him about what he was going to do, and asked him if he could talk to the exec afterward. Bill thought the guy would need some moral support. So later that day, Dave tentatively walked into the guy's office and was surprised to see him excited and pumped up. Bill had indeed delivered the tough message, but the guy felt great about it. Dave went back to Bill's office and took credit for rebuilding the man's confidence, when in fact no damage had been done!

---

## NO GAP BETWEEN STATEMENTS AND FACT

### BE RELENTLESSLY HONEST AND CANDID, COUPLE NEGATIVE FEEDBACK WITH CARING, GIVE FEEDBACK AS SOON AS POSSIBLE, AND IF THE FEEDBACK IS NEGATIVE, DELIVER IT PRIVATELY.

---

## DON'T STICK IT IN THEIR EAR

And when he was finished asking questions and listening, and busting your butt, he usually would *not* tell you what to do. He believed that managers should not walk in with an idea and "stick it in their ear." Don't tell people what to do, tell them stories about why they are doing it.

"I used to describe success and prescribe to everyone how we were going to do it," says Dan Rosensweig. "Bill coached me to tell stories. When people understand the story they can connect to it and figure out what to do. You need to get people to buy in. It's like a running back in football. You don't tell him exactly what route to run. You tell him where the hole is and what's the blocking scheme and let him figure it out."

Jonathan often experienced this as a sort of test: Bill would tell a story and let Jonathan go off and think about it until their next session to see if Jonathan could process and understand the lesson it contained and its implications. Chad Hurley, YouTube cofounder, had the same experience. "It was like sitting with a friend at the Old Pro [the Palo Alto sports bar]," Chad says. "He would talk about things that had happened to him. He wasn't trying to preach, just be present."

Fortunately, Bill expected similar candor in return. Alan Gleicher, who worked with Bill as the head of sales and operations at Intuit, had a simple way of summing up how to be successful with him. "Don't dance. If Bill asks a question and you don't know the answer, don't dance around it. Tell him you don't know!" For Bill, honesty and integrity weren't just about keeping your word and telling the truth; they were also about being forthright. This is critical for effective coaching; a good coach doesn't hide the stuff that's hard to talk about—in fact, a good coach will draw this out. He or she gets at the hard stuff.

Scholars would describe Bill's approach—listening, providing honest feedback, demanding candor—as "relational transparency," which is a core characteristic of "authentic leadership."[13] Wharton professor Adam Grant has another term for it: "disagreeable givers." He notes in an email to us that "we often feel torn between supporting and challenging others. Social scientists reach the same conclusion for leadership as they do for parenting: it's a false dichotomy. You want to be supportive *and* demanding, holding high standards and expectations but giving the encouragement necessary to reach them. Basically, it's tough love. Disagreeable givers are gruff and tough on the surface, but underneath they have others' best interests at heart. They give the critical feedback no one wants to hear but everyone needs to hear."

Research on organizations shows what Bill seemed to know instinctively: that these leadership traits lead to better team performance. One study of a chain of retail stores found that when employees saw their managers as authentic (for example, agreeing that the manager "says exactly what he or she means"), the employees trusted the leaders more, and the stores had higher sales.[14]

---

## DON'T STICK IT IN THEIR EAR

### DON'T TELL PEOPLE WHAT TO DO; OFFER STORIES AND HELP GUIDE THEM TO THE BEST DECISIONS FOR THEM.

---

# BE THE EVANGELIST FOR COURAGE

In 2014, Twitter was negotiating a partnership deal with Google that would allow Google to include tweets in its search results. Dick Costolo, Twitter's CEO at the time, was working with his team on the deal. There were a lot of concerns about the terms, so the team was advocating a smaller deal to test things out first. Dick updated Bill on the progress at his next coaching 1:1.

"This is onesy, twosy stuff," Bill told him. Dick shouldn't nibble around the edges; he should push for the boldest solution possible. If he was going to do something big, there was no way to anticipate all the smaller details and problems, so maybe sign a shorter-term deal. But the main point was to go big. "There's a big idea here! Come up with a more courageous path forward." Dick got the team to be more aggressive, and a few months later they announced a deal to give Google access to Twitter's data stream.

Bill's perspective was that it's a manager's job to push the team to be more courageous. Courage is hard. People are naturally afraid of taking risks for fear of failure. It's the manager's job to push them past their reticence. Shona Brown, a longtime Google executive, calls it being an "evangelist for courage." As a coach, Bill was a never-ending evangelist for courage. As Bill Gurley notes, he "blew confidence into people." He believed you could do things, even when you yourself weren't so sure, always pushing you to go beyond your self-imposed limits. Danny Shader, founder and CEO of PayNearMe, who worked with Bill at GO: "The thing I got the most out of meetings with Bill is courage. I always came away thinking, I can do this. He believed you could do stuff that you didn't believe you could do."

Emil Michael says, "He would always convey boldness to me. It would always give me such a boost. That's one thing

I learned from Bill: be the person who gives energy, not one who takes it away." This quality of constant encouragement, of being the person to give energy, has been shown to be one of the most important aspects of effective coaching.*[15]

Shishir Mehrotra started his first company, Centrata, in 2001. Not long afterward, he got a call from one of his investors. The company was struggling and needed to cut expenses. The investor had gone through the résumés of everyone in the company and chosen the people he felt should be laid off. They were mostly the more junior people in the company; the investor thought the company needed to retain its more experienced people. The problem was, most of the people the investor had selected were Shishir's cofounders. Shishir didn't think letting them go was a smart move, but when pressed by the investor, he did it. Then he called Bill.

Bill was furious. Where was Shishir's courage? "His constant advice to me, even back then, was to trust my instincts," Shishir says. "I was twenty-two years old!" Bill asked Shishir, did he think laying off all the junior staff was the right thing to do? Shishir's answer was no, these people are the cofounders, they care more. The more senior people are more like mercenaries. They'll leave as soon as things go south. Bill coached Shishir to have the courage to follow his instincts, so he turned around and rehired the people he had just laid off. They formed the core of the company for the next several years.

---

* For example, a 2011 study from the Ashridge Business School in the United Kingdom ranks "encouragement" as the third-most-appreciated quality in a coach, behind only listening and understanding.

Conveying boldness was not blind cheerleading on Bill's part. He had the mind-set that most people have value, and he had the experience and a good enough eye for talent that he generally knew what he was talking about. He had such credibility that if he said that you could do something, you believed him, not because he was a cheerleader but because he was a coach and experienced executive. He built his message on your capabilities and progress. This is a key aspect of delivering encouragement as a coach: it needs to be credible.*[16]

And if you believed him, you started to believe in yourself, which of course helped you achieve whatever daunting task lay before you. "He gave me permission to go forth," Alphabet CFO Ruth Porat says. "To have confidence in my judgment."

This confidence is even more important when things are rough. Millard "Mickey" Drexler, the former CEO of J.Crew and Gap, who sat on the Apple board for sixteen years alongside Bill, is a firm believer in the CEO as coach model, particularly in challenging times. When things are bad, "people come into work every day getting beat up. Everyone feels awful. As a leader, you can't fix problems on your own, and you can't fix them when morale is down. So you need to build the confidence of the team."

Bill set high standards for his coachees; he believed they

---

* A 2014 research paper from Y. Joel Wong of Indiana University shows that "perceived trustworthiness of the encourager" is an important characteristic in differentiating effective encouragement from blind cheerleading.

could be great, greater than what they believed. This created an aspiration for each of us, and disappointment when we thought that we were not living up to that aspiration. Bill set the bar higher for us than we set it for ourselves, and when you approach people with that mind-set, they respond.

## BE THE EVANGELIST FOR COURAGE

### BELIEVE IN PEOPLE MORE THAN THEY BELIEVE IN THEMSELVES, AND PUSH THEM TO BE MORE COURAGEOUS.

## FULL IDENTITY FRONT AND CENTER

David Drummond is Alphabet's head of corporate development and legal affairs, and is an African American. "When you come from a background that is not traditional—if you're black—you don't typically fit in," David says. "There is a strong pressure to conform and not show that part of yourself. In Silicon Valley, you are supposed to be either technical or from a fancy business school." Bill Campbell was neither, but he still, as David puts it, "put his full identity front and center."

Bill and David talked about this, with Bill counseling

David that so much about him was where he came from, and that he should hang on to that as a source of motivation and strength. "He made me less self-conscious about the fact that I wasn't the same as everyone. That I was black."

One thing we learned from interviewing people for this book was how much Bill encouraged people to be themselves at work, well before the "bringing your whole self" meme became so popular. This isn't something we ever heard directly from him; white heterosexual males who attended top schools (that is, us) don't typically have issues with being themselves at their workplace. But as a guy from a working-class town, a former football coach with a nontechnical degree who parachuted into Silicon Valley in the early 1980s, Bill had some experience with feeling out of place. Yet he was always fully himself, and he expected no less than that from the people he coached. He felt that when people could be so authentic as to bring their full selves to work, they would be more respected by their colleagues, and would appreciate it more when others did the same.

Brad Smith (former Intuit CEO) and Shellye Archambeau (former CEO of MetricStream) received similar advice from Bill. Brad is from West Virginia and sports a strong accent; early in his career he was advised to get speech training to lose it. He decided not to. "I realized my accent isn't a bug, it's a feature," Brad now says (perfectly mixing Silicon Valley parlance with West Virginia drawl). "People prefer leaders who are different because it makes leadership seem more attainable." Shellye is an African American, and early in her career, when she was in sales at IBM, she tried to shed her cultural background and dress and act like everyone else. Bill helped her past that. "He encouraged me to dress however I felt most comfortable, because people can tell when you're not being yourself," she says. "Then they try to figure out why not, and that breeds distrust."

## FULL IDENTITY FRONT AND CENTER

### PEOPLE ARE MOST EFFECTIVE WHEN THEY CAN BE COMPLETELY THEMSELVES AND BRING THEIR FULL IDENTITY TO WORK.

These are the elements that formed the foundation of Bill's success as an executive coach—and that those who benefited from his coaching took with them when they became coaches to their own colleagues and direct reports, too. He started by building trust, which only deepened over time. He was highly selective in choosing his coachees; he would only coach the coachable, the humble, hungry lifelong learners. He listened intently, without distraction. He usually didn't tell you what to do; rather, he shared stories and let you draw conclusions. He gave, and demanded, complete candor. And he was an evangelist for courage, by showing inordinate confidence and setting aspirations high.

All of these created a remarkable environment when you were in the room with him: it was an atmosphere dedicated to making you better. As former CEO of eBay John Donahoe says, "It wasn't so much about the advice and insight he gave me. With Bill you close your eyes and it's more about who he was. I felt it more than I heard it."

CHAPTER 4

# Team First

When Google went public, in August 2004, it created two classes of stock. Class A shares were the ones sold to the public, each share coming with traditional voting rights: one share equals one vote. But class B shares were different: each share came with ten votes. Class B shares were not sold publicly and were held by Google insiders, such as cofounders Larry Page and Sergey Brin, and CEO Eric. This "dual class" structure ensured that Google's founders and executive team retained control of the company. This structure was unusual at the time and highly controversial, stirring public debate in the months leading up to the IPO.*

---

* Early examples of companies with dual class share structures include Ford, the New York Times Company, and Berkshire Hathaway. Since

To Larry and Sergey, the structure was a critical element of their vision for the company. They admired Warren Buffett and had become knowledgeable about the dual class stock structure that his company Berkshire Hathaway employed. They had always considered Google as much an institution as a business. They fervently believed in thinking long term, making big bets and big investments in those bets, without having to consider the quarterly ups and downs of public markets. They were concerned that Google would lose this "think big" propensity once it was a public company, and they saw the dual class stock structure as a way to guard against that happening. Their interests would always be aligned with that of shareholders, they reasoned, because long-term thinking and investing was the best way to maximize value for everyone.

Eric found himself at the center of this debate. After many hours talking with the founders, he became convinced that theirs was the best approach. He believed it would keep Google on track not just in its current businesses but in its broader mission of organizing the world's information, and it would actually lead to the creation of greater shareholder value than the traditional structure. He made this case to the board, but there was still a lot of open discussion.

At the same time, some board members had been mulling over the idea of bringing in a new chairman of the board, someone who was more independent of the company, and the

---

2004, structures with differing voting rights for different stock classes have become more commonplace, being adopted by Facebook, LinkedIn, and Snap, among others.

discussion on the dual stock classes pushed them even further in that direction. They asked Eric if he would step aside as chairman. He would remain as CEO.

Eric was hurt by this stance. He felt he had done a good job in his three years as chairman and CEO, and, as far as he knew, the board agreed. He had earned the trust of the founders and employees, the company had performed very well, and they were about to go public. And for that they wanted to remove him as chairman? He got on a call with Bill and gave his perspective on the situation.

"What are you going to do?" Bill asked.

In a moment full of pride and hurt, Eric said, "I'm going to quit Google."

"Okay," Bill said. "When?"

At that moment, as the coach of Google's executive team, Bill became a critical player in the future of the company. The greatest team in technology was about to break up. Bill couldn't let it happen. The meeting with the board where all this would be decided—where Eric was going to step down not just as chairman, but maybe as CEO, too—was on Thursday, a couple of days hence. Bill got to work.

Bill Campbell was a coach of teams. He built them, shaped them, put the right players in the right positions (and removed the wrong players from the wrong positions), cheered them on, and kicked them in their collective butt when they were underperforming. He knew, as he often said, that "you can't get anything done without a team." This is an obvious point in the realm of sports, but it's often underappreciated in business. "You can only really succeed and accomplish things through the collective, the common purpose," Lee C. Bollinger says.

"There are so many ways in which people don't understand this, and even when they do understand it, they don't know how to do it. That's where Bill's genius was."

Bill's guiding principle was that the team is paramount, and the most important thing he looked for and expected in people was a "team-first" attitude. Teams are not successful unless every member is loyal and will, when necessary, subjugate their personal agenda to that of the team. That the team wins has to be the most important thing. Perhaps Charles Darwin said it best in his book *The Descent of Man*: "A tribe including many members who, from possessing in a high degree the spirit of patriotism, fidelity, obedience, courage, and sympathy, were always ready to aid one another, and to sacrifice themselves for the common good, would be victorious over most other tribes; and this would be natural selection."[1]

Back in 2004, Bill correctly assessed that feelings were rubbed raw over the pending IPO, the discussions on how to structure the company, and the idea that Eric step down as chairman. He understood that Eric was hurt, but he also knew that the team needed him to stay. He also felt that Eric was the best person to be the company's chairman, at that point and for the foreseeable future. So he thought about the situation and called Eric back the next day. You can't leave, the team needs you, he stated. How about if you step down as chairman for now, and remain as CEO? And then at some point, not too far from now, Bill would see to it that Eric got reinstated as chairman.

He'd offered a reasonable compromise and appealed to Eric's loyalty to Google. This was not a fight to have today, he told Eric. Your pride is getting in the way of what's best for the company, and for you.

Eric saw that Bill was right, and he had no doubt that Bill could implement what he was proposing, so Eric agreed. Together they talked through how the board meeting the next day would go, and by the time Thursday rolled around, Eric was well prepared. He stepped down as chairman and stayed on as CEO. Later, in 2007, he was reinstated as chairman, a role he held until April 2011. He was executive chairman from that date until January 2018.

Many people might look at Eric's short-lived decision to leave Google as completely crazy. Look how much stock he would be leaving behind! But in teams, and particularly high-performing teams, other things matter, too. It's not just about money! Purpose, pride, ambition, ego: these are vital motivators as well and must be considered by any manager or coach. Bill knew that he had to appeal to Eric both emotionally and rationally. His suggested compromise worked.

At the time he proposed the compromise, Bill did not have everyone's agreement that Eric would be reinstated as chairman down the road. He simply knew that it was the right thing to do for the company, and that, as the coach, he had the influence to make things like that happen. Bill's integrity and his long record of sound judgment were paramount. When the time was right, when the IPO was done and emotions had simmered down, Bill would make the case to reinstate Eric as chairman. Which is exactly what happened.

This was an example of high-stakes team building, with a multibillion-dollar IPO at stake and investors, founders, and executives debating difficult issues. But it is in precisely these situations that a team coach is needed the most, someone who can see past individual egos and understand the value that all of the members, combined, create. Team building is vital at every company, and the principles Bill espoused apply at every level of an organization. But it gets a lot harder to hold a team together at senior levels in companies, where egos and ambitions are considerable.

Senior executives may have access to individual executive coaching, but team coaches at that level are more rare. After all, all-star teams may have coaches, but they aren't really coaching—they usually just sit back and enjoy the show! So why should executive teams, which consist of presumably the most talented people in the company, need a coach? "It was bizarre to me when I first joined the company," Patrick Pichette says. "You have all these amazing people at Google. Why would they need a coach?"

In fact, it's nearly impossible to overstate Bill's influence in nurturing the Google management team during the company's formative years, an influence that continued until he passed away. As Omid Kordestani, former Google head of sales, puts it: "What was very special about Google was the community aspect of the senior team. Bill was the glue in that process."

So as a coach of teams, what would Bill do? His first instinct was always to work the team, not the problem. In other words, he focused on the team's dynamics, not on trying to solve the team's particular challenges. That was their job. His job was team building, assessing people's talents, and finding the doers. He ran toward the biggest problems, the stinkers that fester and cause tension. He focused on winning but winning right, and he doubled down on his core values when things turned south. And he brought resolution by filling the gaps between people, listening, observing, and then seeking people out in behind-the-scenes conversations that brought teams together.

"You always had the sense he was building a team," says Sheryl Sandberg. "With Bill, it wasn't executive coaching or career coaching. It was never just about me. It was always about the team."

## WORK THE TEAM, THEN THE PROBLEM

At a Google meeting a few years ago, the group was discussing an issue related to costs in some of the developing businesses. Ram Shriram raised concerns: the numbers were getting big! Shouldn't we get more details on how we are working on this? There was some back-and-forth, then Bill spoke up. Don't worry, he said, we have the right team in place. They are working the problem.

"I learned something from that," Ram says. "Bill didn't work the problem first, he worked the team. We didn't talk about the problem analytically. We talked about the people on the team and if they could get it done."

As managers, we tend to focus on the problem at hand. What is the situation? What are the issues? What are the options? And so on. These are valid questions, but the coach's instinct is to lead with a more fundamental one. Who was working on the problem? Was the right team in place? Did they have what they needed to succeed? "When I became CEO of Google," Sundar Pichai says, "Bill advised me that at that level, more than ever before, you need to bet on people. Choose your team. Think much harder about that."

Bill helped us employ this approach in a problem that arose in 2010. Apple (and in particular, Steve Jobs) believed that Google's Android operating system violated patents that Apple had developed for the iPhone. They sued Google's business partners, the manufacturers of Android phones. This wasn't just a business or a legal problem to Bill—it was personal. He was close friends with Jobs and a member of Apple's board—as well as an informal but influential coach to Google's leadership team. It was like his two children were fighting, with much more at stake than a favorite toy.

Bill's approach was to focus on the team, not the problem. He never even offered an opinion on the relative merits of each side's case, even though he was quite knowledgeable about the issues and the phone features in question. He did, however, counsel Eric to put the right guy in charge of talking to Apple: Alan Eustace. Alan became the chief diplomat interfacing with Apple. It became his job to ensure that the relationship between the companies didn't implode.

Much later in Bill's career, Google was planning an important change to its corporate structure. The company was forming a new holding company, to be called Alphabet, and moving some of its most speculative efforts (called "other bets") out into separate companies. This new organization was a major shift in the operating structure and management culture; Sundar Pichai was being promoted to run Google, with Larry Page moving over to become CEO of Alphabet. Meanwhile, the company's head of sales, Nikesh Arora, had left, creating a big hole in one of the key leadership positions. The company contacted Omid Kordestani, its first head of sales. Would he be interested in coming back?

"It was clear at that point that we would be moving to Alphabet, and that Sundar would be CEO of Google," Omid says, "but it wasn't clear how we would get there. There were so many complex steps involved." When he talked to Bill, they didn't talk about the operational changes or any of the tactics or strategy involved. They talked about the team. Bill wanted someone who cared about the company and its people to help with the transition, which described Omid perfectly. "Care for the team like that is unusual at that level," Omid says. "It tends to be pretty cutthroat. But not for Bill. The management team was his primary love."

---

## WORK THE TEAM, THEN THE PROBLEM

### WHEN FACED WITH A PROBLEM OR OPPORTUNITY, THE FIRST STEP IS TO ENSURE THE RIGHT TEAM IS IN PLACE AND WORKING ON IT.

---

# PICK THE RIGHT PLAYERS

"If you're running a company, you have to surround yourself with really, really good people," Bill said. Not one of his most surprising statements: it is a tired business mantra to always hire people smarter than yourself. "Everybody that is managing a function on behalf of the CEO ought to be better at that function than the CEO. Some of the time, they are going to be wearing their HR hat or their IT hat, but most of the time you want them to be wearing their company hat. These are all smart people that have great capabilities, and what you want to get is the best idea that comes from that group."

Bill looked for four characteristics in people. The person has to be smart, not necessarily academically but more from the standpoint of being able to get up to speed quickly in different areas and then make connections. Bill called this the ability to make "far analogies." The person has to work hard, and has to have high integrity. Finally, the person should have that hard-to-define characteristic: grit. The ability to get knocked down and have the passion and perseverance to get up and go at it again.

He would tolerate a lot of other faults if he thought a person had those four characteristics. When he interviewed job candidates to assess these points, he wouldn't just ask about what a person did, he would ask how they did it. If the person said they "led a project that led to revenue growth," asking *how* they achieved that growth will tell you a lot about how they were involved in the project. Were they hands-on? Were they doers? Did they build the team? He would listen for the pronouns: does the person say "I" (could signify a me-first mentality) or "we" (a potential indicator of a team player)?*[2]

A big turnoff for Bill was if they were no longer learning. Do they have more answers than questions? That's a bad sign!

He looked for commitment, to the cause and not just to their own success. Team first! You need to find, as Sundar Pichai says, "people who understand that their success depends on working well together, that there's give-and-take—people who put the company first." Whenever Sundar and Bill found people like that, Sundar says, "we would cherish them."

But how do you know when you have found such a person? Keep note of the times when they give up things, and when they are excited for someone else's success. Sundar notes that "sometimes decisions come up and people have to give up things. I overindex on those signals when people give something up.† And also when someone is excited because something else is working well in the company. It isn't related to them, but they are excited. I watch for that. Like when you see a player on the bench cheering for someone else on the

---

* This is the rare instance where available research does not bear out Bill's principle. As James Pennebaker states in his book *The Secret Life of Pronouns*, use of "I" vs. "we" is not a good indicator of whether a person is a team player. Rather, it is an indicator of status. Lower-status people (for example, individual contributors in a company, first-year students in a university) use "I" more often, while higher-status people (executives, professors) use "we" more. We are not amused.

† *Overindex* is geek-speak for "pay a lot of attention to."

team, like Steph Curry jumping up and down when Kevin Durant hits a big shot. You can't fake that."*

In 2011, Eric stepped down as Google CEO. In the ensuing reorganization, Jonathan's job as head of products was eliminated. He was considering a few options, including running the Enterprise business (now Google Cloud, a multibillion-dollar division), but decided to decline them all. He felt hurt by the reorg and considered these other jobs a demotion. Bill was so disappointed; Jonathan was putting his bruised ego ahead of what was best for the Google team (and, in fact, himself). He was making a "mistake born of ego and emotion," and Bill thought Jonathan maybe should consider removing his head from his ass.

Bill suggested that Jonathan take more time to consider his decision, and he continued to meet with him on a regular basis. With Bill's help, Jonathan later found his way back into the Google fold by taking on other roles. Bill didn't give up on him, but he also never let him forget how he had let the team down. This was a vivid and personal lesson: when change happens, the priority has to be what is best for the team.

Bill valued courage: the willingness to take risks and the willingness to stand up for what's right for the team, which may entail taking a personal risk. Earlier in his Google career, before he became CEO, Sundar Pichai would often speak up when he felt something wasn't the right choice, both to us and later to Larry Page when he was CEO. That takes some

---

* Steph Curry and Kevin Durant are stars on the NBA's Golden State Warriors, who had just won their third title in four years when Sundar (a big Warriors fan) said this.

guts, but as Sundar says, "Bill always appreciated it when I spoke my mind about difficult issues because he knew I cared about the company and the products, and that's where I was coming from."

Sundar respects the same in others when he sees it today. "There are people who are team players and really care about the company. When they speak up, it matters a lot to me because I know they are coming from the right place."

Bill was attracted to people who were "difficult"—more outspoken in their opinions, occasionally abrasive, not afraid to buck trends or the crowd. "Like diamonds that are somehow misshapen," is how Alan Eustace puts it. Bill's friendship with Steve Jobs was a testament to this, as was his long partnership with other founders: Larry Page and Sergey Brin of Google, Scott Cook of Intuit. Not an easygoing person among them! We don't think Bill sought this out as a personality trait, but he tolerated it and even embraced it. Whereas others might find this type of person difficult, Bill found these people interesting and worth developing, sometimes helping them smooth away rough edges. The most effective coaches tolerate and even encourage some level of eccentricity and "prickliness" among their team members. Outstanding performers, from athletes to founders to business executives, are often "difficult." You want them on your team.

Sheryl Sandberg says that the first time she met Bill, during her first week at Google in late 2001, he asked her, what do you do here? At the time, Sheryl had been hired with the title of "business unit general manager," a position that didn't exist before she arrived. There were, in fact, no business units, so she had nothing to manage. She answered by saying that she used to be at the Treasury Department. He stopped her: okay, but what do you do *here*? This time, she replied with ideas of what she thought she might do. Bill wasn't satisfied: but what do you do here? Sheryl finally copped to the truth: so far, she didn't do anything. "I learned an incredibly important lesson," she says. "It's not what you used to do, it's not what you think, it's what you do every day." This is perhaps the most important characteristic Bill looked for in his players: people who show up, work hard, and have an impact every day. *Doers*.

As you evaluate people, it's important to consider how they fit in the team and the company. People, especially in Silicon Valley, tend to look for "superheroes," people with superior smarts and savvy who can do it all and be the best at everything. This is magnified at companies' senior levels. As Philipp Schindler says, "Bill made the point that you don't want to staff a team with just quarterbacks; you need to pay a lot of attention to the team composition and have a diverse set of different talents smartly woven together." All people have their limitations; what's important is to understand them individually, to identify what makes them different, and then to see how you can help them mesh with the rest of the team. Bill appreciated high cognitive abilities, but he also understood the value of soft skills, like empathy, that aren't always valued in businesses, especially tech ones. At Google, he helped us learn to appreciate that this combination—smarts and hearts—creates better managers.

He did not overemphasize experience. He looked at skills and mind-set, and he could project what you could become. This is a coach's talent, the ability to see a player's potential, not just current performance. Maybe not completely accurately: as Stanford professor Carol Dweck points out in her 2006 book, *Mindset*, someone's true potential is unknowable, since "it's impossible to foresee what can be accomplished with years of passion, toil, and training."[3] But even without that accuracy, you can bet on potential enough to avoid writing off people solely because they lack experience. The general tendency is to hire for experience: I'm hiring for job X, so I want someone who has years of experience doing job X. If you are creating a high-performing team and building for the future, you need to hire for potential as well as experience.

Picking the right players can also entail reconsidering who else within the company should be on the team. When Jonathan ran the product team at Google, his staff included several product management leaders. But because of how the company was organized, it did not include engineering leaders. This led to some conflict when it came time to allocate and assign people and resources; the product leads didn't always agree with the engineering leads. Jonathan's staff meetings often involved a lot of argument about these decisions, and some complaining about the absent engineering leads.

Bill's counsel to Jonathan was simple: add some players to the team. Jonathan should invite the engineering leads to his staff meeting. Not to just one meeting, but permanently. Then force the discussion of plans with them, air the arguments, and get everyone to buy in on whatever decisions were made. The purpose of the meetings was not for Jonathan to demonstrate command of topics discussed and tell people what to do (which, as Bill observed, was sometimes

Jonathan's practice); it was to get the team to gel. Bringing in the people who were a focal point of dissension was the only way to do that. Sure, there were still plenty of arguments, but because more of the players were in the room, they got resolved more quickly, which helped create stronger relationships across groups.

Bill started to show a knack for picking players early in his business career. Eric Johnson was a colleague of Bill's at Kodak. Eric says that at the time Kodak was very profitable, so it wasn't too concerned with getting rid of mediocre performers. Bill wasn't one to make heads roll, either—he got better at dealing with poor performers later on, when he had to as CEO of Intuit. However, at Kodak he developed a talent for finding the "doers" in any department and getting those people talking. This isn't always easy in a large company, but Bill would look for those same characteristics he looked for in candidates: smarts, hard work, integrity, grit. And then he would figure out ways to formally or informally bring those people together to talk and make stuff happen, around a particular project or problem.

"People would look forward to the meeting with Bill," Eric recounts, "because when Campbell ran a meeting or brought a group together, the environment was results oriented, everyone participated and contributed, and they actually enjoyed the meeting. It was positive and fun to be part of a team."

---

## PICK THE RIGHT PLAYERS

### THE TOP CHARACTERISTICS TO LOOK FOR ARE SMARTS AND HEARTS: THE ABILITY TO LEARN FAST, A WILLINGNESS TO WORK HARD, INTEGRITY, GRIT, EMPATHY, AND A TEAM-FIRST ATTITUDE.

---

## PAIR PEOPLE

As we noted earlier, Bill highly valued peer relationships. An important, often overlooked, aspect of team building is developing relationships within the team. This can happen organically, but it is important enough that it should not be left to chance. So Bill looked for any opportunity to pair people up. Take a couple of people who don't usually work together, assign them a task, project, or decision, and let them work on it on their own. This develops trust between the two people, usually regardless of the nature of the work.[*][4]

This was one of Bill's first suggestions to Jonathan. After sitting in on a couple of his staff meetings, Bill told Jonathan

---

* A 1995 study by Daniel McAllister of Georgetown University shows that trust increases with the frequency of interaction between a manager and a peer.

that he needed to work more on coaching people and pairing them up on things. Don't just be a dictator assigning tasks, pair people up! So from that point forward, for projects such as preparing material for public events like earnings calls, producing team off-sites, working on compensation and promotion ladders, and developing internal tools, Jonathan stopped dictating and started pairing people up. The results: better decisions, stronger team.

Bill would coach Jonathan to do this himself. When Patrick Pichette joined Google as CFO, Bill asked Jonathan to seek him out and mentor him on the ways of the company. This was helpful to Patrick, but it also helped create a new trusted pair relationship on Eric's management team, which was the actual objective. The deliverable matters, but what matters just as much is the opportunity for the pair of teammates to work together on something and get to know and trust each other. That is invaluable to the team's success.

---

**PAIR PEOPLE**

PEER RELATIONSHIPS
ARE CRITICAL AND OFTEN
OVERLOOKED, SO SEEK
OPPORTUNITIES TO PAIR PEOPLE
UP ON PROJECTS OR DECISIONS.

---

## THE PEER FEEDBACK SURVEY

B ill felt so strongly about the importance of peer relationships that he helped design a peer feedback survey
we used for years at Google. Respondents gave feedback
about colleagues, and the results provided a good picture
of how well a person was performing in the eyes of their
peers, the most important evaluators, in Bill's opinion.

The survey was initially designed to elicit opinions on
four aspects of a person's performance: job performance,
relationship with peer groups, management and leadership, and innovation. Later Bill insisted that it be expanded to include a question about people's behavior in
meetings. He was dismayed by how many people chose
to be on their phones or laptops in meetings! We added a
question about collaboration as well, and a set of questions
on product vision that went just to product leaders. Here is
the complete survey:

# CORE ATTRIBUTES

**For the past 12 months, to what extent do you agree/ disagree that each person:**

- Displayed extraordinary in-role performance.
- Exemplified world-class leadership.
- Achieved outcomes that were in the best interest of both Google as a whole and his/her organization.
- Expanded the boundaries of what is possible for Google through innovation and/or application of best practices.
- Collaborated effectively with peers (for example, worked well together, resolved barriers/issues with others) and championed the same in his/her team.
- Contributed effectively during senior team meetings (for example, was prepared, participated actively, listened well, was open and respectful to others, disagreed constructively).

## PRODUCT LEADER ATTRIBUTES

For the past 12 months, to what extent do you agree/ disagree that each person demonstrated exemplary leadership in the following areas:

- Product Vision
- Product Quality
- Product Execution

## OPEN-TEXT QUESTIONS

- What differentiates each SVP and makes him/her effective today?
- What advice would you give each SVP to be more effective and/or have greater impact?

# GET TO THE TABLE

In the 1980s, the majority of executives at technology companies were men; there were very few women.[*5] Deb Biondolillo was one of those women, the head of U.S. human resources at Apple. Still, when the weekly CEO staff meeting rolled around, Deb would sit in the row of chairs along the wall, not at the table. Bill couldn't stand this. "What are you doing back there?" he would ask Deb. "Get to the table!" Finally, one day Deb got to the meeting early and nervously grabbed a seat at the table. The other guys filtered in, and one of them, Al Eisenstat, ended up sitting next to Deb. Al was a dynamic executive, Apple's general counsel, and one of its heads of marketing prior to Bill, a powerful man who was instrumental to Apple's early growth. He was also well known for being rather gruff. When he took his seat that day, he was surprised to see Deb sitting next to him, at the table. "What are you doing here?" he barked.

"Going to the meeting," she replied, with more confidence than she felt.

"Al looked at me for a few seconds," Deb says. "Then he looked over at Bill. That's when I knew it would be okay. Bill would back me up."

More than anyone we have ever encountered in our careers, Bill was an advocate for women being "at the table."

---

* Three decades later, women still constitute a minority of executives in technology. A 2016 U.S. Equal Employment Opportunity Commission report states that 20 percent of high-tech execs are women, while a 2018 Entelo Women in Tech report pegs the number at 10 percent.

He believed in diversity on teams well before it was a common topic. This is counterintuitive: Bill swore, loved football and a good dirty joke, perfected the guys' trip, and loved beer. He was a real guy's guy. Most of this "guy" activity, except for the swearing, took place outside the workplace, but not entirely. And it likely made at least some of the women around Bill feel excluded from time to time; some women may not feel comfortable telling jokes over beers at a sports bar. Yet all of the women we talked to about Bill felt comfortable with his style, because they saw firsthand that Bill was a straight shooter who delivered tough messages with respect, warmth, and candor.

We learned early on from Bill that when it came to creating teams, you have to put your bias blinders on (and that we all have biases). To him it was simple. Winning depends on having the best team, and the best teams include more women. A pair of 2010 studies bear Bill out on this point. They examined collective intelligence in teams: why are some teams "smarter" than the sum of their individual IQs? The answer is threefold: on the most effective teams everyone contributes rather than one or two people dominating discussions, people on those teams are better at reading complex emotional states, and . . . the teams have more women. This can be partly explained by the fact that women tend to be better at reading emotional states than men.[6] So Bill always pushed us to consider women for any senior positions; he believed "you can always find a woman for a job, it may just take a little longer." He helped recruit them when he could, such as when he got Ruth Porat to come on board as Google's CFO in 2015.

He pushed the women he coached to be more aggressive

in seeking bigger roles and more P&L responsibility, particularly in jobs outside of "typical" female areas such as HR or PR.* He connected successful women he knew with other successful women. He had zero tolerance for any gender bias in business conversations.

Bill helped bring Eve Burton to the Intuit board and worked with her extensively in her role as SVP and general counsel at Hearst, the media conglomerate. He coached Eve on various content deals she was negotiating, and the two of them collaborated on a journalism and technology partnership between Columbia and Stanford. But none of this work was more important to Bill than the HearstLab, a business "greenhouse" for women-led companies that Eve started at Hearst under Bill's prodding and tutelage. Those companies now have a collective value of more than $200 million! "It was the last thing he pushed me to do," Eve says. "His vision was to give women a place to seed their companies and make them successful."

And a place to get some grass stains, too. One day, Diane Greene was attending an Intuit board meeting when she and Bill started chatting about their kids. Diane's son was playing flag football at his middle school, and her daughter, in fifth grade, had complained that it wasn't fair that the boys got to play football and the girls didn't. Bill told Diane to come to Sacred Heart, the private school in nearby Atherton, on Thursday afternoon, and to bring her daughter. He didn't say

---

* P&L is profit and loss, having financial responsibility for a business unit or company. HR is human resources; PR is public relations.

why. When Diane and her daughter arrived, they saw a bunch of middle school girls practicing football. Bill was on the field coaching them, with as much energy (and colorful language) as he did the boys' team. "He wanted her to see that girls can play football, too," Diane says. "He was coaching a football team; it didn't matter that it was girls. He found the time to fit it in and hardly even talked about it."

He took time to talk to adult women's teams, too. For example, not long after she became CEO of MetricStream, Shellye Archambeau formed a group of women CEOs to support and mentor each other. She invited Bill to come to one meeting, and they all enjoyed it so much that it became a regular event. They would gather in the conference room at Bill's office in Palo Alto and spend a couple of hours talking about a particular topic du jour. Bill prepared for and usually orchestrated the meeting. He didn't tell the women what to do; rather, he told stories about his experiences and asked questions.

In most of the discussions, the fact that the CEOs around the table were all women didn't even come up and wasn't particularly relevant. However, when diversity did come up, or when some of the women related some of the biases they had experienced, Bill always got frustrated. He reminded them to think of the other women around the table when opportunities come up. This can be a problem: a 2017 *Harvard Business Review* article notes that sometimes members of minority groups hesitate to bring other members of that group into their organizations because they don't want to be perceived as giving special treatment, and they worry that the people they bring in might not "make the grade."[7] So Bill always told Shellye's group that if they were looking for board members, look around the group first.

Shellye thought of Bill when she launched a diversity program for women at her company's office in Bangalore, India. They had more than a thousand people there, 30 percent of whom were women, at the time a high percentage for a tech company in India. Not long after launching the program she traveled to the office to check in on business and see how the initiative was going. She gathered the diversity committee and the leadership team into a conference room that was a bit too small. There were not enough chairs at the table for everyone. Shellye noticed that the women who filed in all took the chairs around the edge of the room; the men automatically sat at the table. She stopped them and instructed the women to sit at the table and the men to move to the outer chairs. Then she proceeded with the meeting.

When it was over, she asked the men how it felt to be sitting against the wall, not at the table. Um, weird and uncomfortable, they responded.

Exactly, she replied. To truly include everyone, everyone needs to be at the table.

---

## GET TO THE TABLE

### WINNING DEPENDS ON HAVING THE BEST TEAM, AND THE BEST TEAMS HAVE MORE WOMEN.

---

## SOLVE THE BIGGEST PROBLEM

There is another issue with the largely cognitive approach to management, which we had big-time at Google. Smart, analytical people, especially ones steeped in computer science and mathematics as we were, will tend to assume that data and other empirical evidence can solve all problems. Quants or techies with this worldview tend to see the inherently messy, emotional tension that's always present in teams of humans as inconvenient and irrational—an irritant that will surely be resolved in the course of a data-driven decision process. Of course, humans don't always work that way. Things come up, tensions arise, and they don't naturally go away. People do their best to avoid talking about these situations, because they're awkward. Which makes it worse.

When that happens, people refer to the "elephant in the room": the big problem that overshadows everything but that no one acknowledges. As former Avon CEO Andrea Jung says, "With Bill there was never an elephant in the room." Or, more accurately, there might have been an elephant, but it wasn't hiding in the corner. Bill wouldn't allow that. He brought the thing front and center.

"It's a football mentality," Shona Brown points out. "Where's the weakest link on the offensive line, or the defensive secondary?" Throughout her tenure at Google, Shona worked weekly with Bill tackling numerous operational issues, many of which were lurking like elephants in the corner. The company was just growing so fast, well ahead of any semblance of process. Bill's approach, Shona says, was always to tackle the hardest problem first. "You have to address that first."

A litmus test for when issues have simmered for too long, a way to spot the elephant, is if the team can't even have honest conversations about them. This is where the coach comes in, as a "tension spotter."

Of course, another word for tension is *politics*. When you hear people saying that things are getting "political," that often means that problems have arisen because the data or process hasn't led to the best decision. At that point, personalities take over. As we discussed earlier, this was anathema to Bill. "For us, political stuff is very toxic," he wrote Jonathan. "We have managed to become a big company with a wonderful absence of politics." The reason we accomplished that, he failed to mention, was his own diligence in tackling the toughest, ugliest problems head-on. He would, as former Google head of communications Rachel Whetstone says, "beat the politics out of the situation" by bringing up the problem clearly, then forcing everyone to focus on it.

There was one situation we had a few years ago where two different product leaders were arguing about which team should manage a particular group of products. Both could legitimately argue that the products belonged on their team. For a while, this was treated as a technical discussion, where data and logic would eventually determine which way to go. But that didn't happen, the problem festered, and tensions rose. It was causing problems within the teams, and with external partners as well. Who was in control?

This is when Bill got involved. There had to be a difficult

meeting where one exec would win and the other would lose. Bill made the meeting happen; he spotted a fundamental tension that was not getting resolved and forced the issue. He didn't have a clear opinion on how to resolve the matter, on which team the product belonged, he simply knew we had to decide one way or another, now. It was one of the most heated meetings we've had, but it had to happen.

---

## SOLVE THE BIGGEST PROBLEM

### IDENTIFY THE BIGGEST PROBLEM, THE "ELEPHANT IN THE ROOM," BRING IT FRONT AND CENTER, AND TACKLE IT FIRST.

---

## DON'T LET THE BITCH SESSIONS LAST

The launch day of Apple's second-generation iPhone, the iPhone 3G, did not go well. Each new phone that was sold was required to connect to Apple servers in order to be activated and functional. But the morning the phones went on sale, July 11, 2008, the servers ran into technical issues and went down. People could buy new phones but couldn't activate them. Furthermore, anyone who had an older version iPhone and tried to upgrade to the new iOS operating system (the first to support the App Store) found that their phones were rendered inoperable in the process. In techie jargon, their phones were "bricked."

At Apple headquarters in Cupertino, Eddy Cue and his team gathered around the table in a conference room, trying to figure out what to do. It was "mass chaos, my worst day at Apple," Eddy says. "All of these issues are coming in, we're trying to figure out what the hell is going on, what are the issues? There was a ton of negativity in the room, people had been lining up all night and we couldn't sell any phones!" The negativity, Eddy realized, was an issue itself. "We had to get down to focus, get our team thinking in the right way, stop worrying about selling phones, and worry instead about fixing the right problems."

Which is what they did. The first step was to take down the iOS update so that people would stop trying to upgrade their original iPhones. And then they got to work on getting their servers up and running, which they did a couple of hours later. Bill Campbell wasn't involved in this situation, but his influence was felt. Bill always made sure that problems were aired completely and transparently. And then, once that was accomplished, he moved on.

"That's one of the big things he taught me," Eddy says. "When it gets to the negative, get it out, get to the issues, but don't let the damn meeting dwell on that. Don't let bitch sessions last for very long." Psychologists would call this approach "problem-focused coping," in contrast to "emotion-focused coping." The latter may be more appropriate when facing a problem that can't be solved, but in a business context focusing on and venting emotions needs to happen quickly, so more energy is directed to solutions.[8]

Bill and the Apple board had plenty of chances to practice this approach in the days after Steve Jobs returned as CEO in 1997. It's easy to forget how Apple, now one of the most successful and valuable companies in the world, was nearly bankrupt when Jobs came back. There were some tough times then, and even later, after the success of the iMac, iPod, iPhone, and iPad, some very challenging issues. Bill's approach was always to be levelheaded and constructive, to immediately focus on what they were going to do about it. Andrea Jung, who joined the Apple board in 2008, calls it "learning forward." Not what happened and who's to blame, but what are we going to do about it?

One way Bill was able to accomplish this trick was by staying relentlessly positive. Negative situations can be infectious, people get cynical, optimism fades. "In those early years we had some tough times," Eddy says, "but Bill was by far the most positive board member we had." It would be easy to dismiss this attitude as mere cheerleading, except that he was also relentless in identifying and addressing problems, which cheerleaders don't do. Studies show that positive leadership makes it easier to solve problems, so Bill would praise teams and people, give them a hug, and clap them on the shoulder to boost their confidence and comfort. Then, when he asked the tough questions, everyone understood that he was on their side, and that he was pushing on things because he wanted them to be better, to be successful. He would always get to the heart of a problem, but in a positive way.[9]

Again, we feel the influence of coaching sports at work here. When we leave the office behind and go coach our kids' soccer or baseball teams, we are always taught the value of "positive coaching," of leading with praise and then following with constructive feedback. But when we get back to work, we forget all that and rip into people. We aren't suggesting that everyone start treating their teams like kids on a playground, but Bill's approach demonstrates that the same basics work even at the highest levels of an organization.

---

## DON'T LET THE BITCH SESSIONS LAST

### AIR ALL THE NEGATIVE ISSUES, BUT DON'T DWELL ON THEM. MOVE ON AS FAST AS POSSIBLE.

---

## WINNING RIGHT

In sports, coaches and players talk about a "culture of winning" and the dynasties that have it. Discussion of the greatest sports dynasties must include the Boston Celtics (eight straight NBA championships from 1959 to 1966), São Paulo's Santos FC (eleven titles from 1955 to 1969), UCLA Bruins men's basketball (ten titles from 1964 to 1975), Manchester United (twelve titles from 1992 to 2011), and the New England Patriots and San Francisco 49ers (both with five Super

Bowl wins, the Niners in the 1980s and '90s and the Patriots from 2002 to 2017). Here are some other numbers that rank right up there: ten league titles in fourteen years. This is what Bill achieved with the Sacred Heart middle school flag football team. Sacred Heart is a private school in Atherton, California, one of the wealthiest zip codes in the United States. Bill turned it into a football dynasty. He would tell the kids, you aren't the rich kids from Atherton, you're the tough kids from Sacred Heart.

You can't talk about coaching—or leading a company—without talking about winning. That's what the good coaches do. That's what great leaders do. Bill didn't approach coaching at Sacred Heart any differently because it was middle school, or because it was an exclusive private school. Those things didn't matter. It was still football, and you still played to win. He demanded commitment, passion, and above all, loyalty, just like in his business life. Sometimes a parent would come to him and explain that their son or daughter would be late to practice because he or she was playing soccer or some other sport. Bill's reply was, that's fine, and he was sure that their child would fare quite well . . . on the B team. They wouldn't be playing on the A squad. Football would not be a second priority for any of his players, and no one got special treatment to accommodate an interest outside the team.

He demanded the same level of commitment from himself and his other coaches (all volunteers with demanding jobs). Every Tuesday and Thursday afternoon in the fall, you would find Bill on the Sacred Heart football field, leading practice. Most people knew not to call Bill during those hours, but at least one person did not. Occasionally Bill's phone would ring during practice and he would take it out of his pocket just long enough to see who was calling, and for the kids to get a glimpse at the caller ID. Then Bill would put the phone back in his pocket, letting the call from Steve Jobs go unanswered. "There was nothing cooler than knowing that for that hour at practice, we were the most important thing to him," one of his players says. "We had his *full* attention."

(Sometimes the young players had his attention even when he wasn't with them. One time Bill came to a practice with a few plays that he had just created for the upcoming game. He had spent the day at a meeting at Google, he explained, and had drawn up the plays during the presentations.)

Still, winning wasn't everything to Bill. Winning *right* was. He would often say he turned to business because he wasn't a very good football coach ("Have you seen my record?"), which is debatable. But what's not debatable is his ability to instill a culture of winning, and winning right. This is what Bill instilled at Sacred Heart, Google, and all the other companies he worked with. Todd Bradley, a former Hewlett-Packard executive who worked extensively with Bill, says that the biggest lesson he learned from him was about "the humanity of winning," by which he means winning as a team (not as individuals) and winning ethically. Whether in business or in sports, it's amazing what can be accomplished if you don't care who gets the credit.

What's remarkable to us, as we talked to numerous people who didn't know Bill as a businessman but as a football coach, is that he treated his middle school football players the same way he treated his executive coachees (like us). The commitment and loyalty. The intolerance for lapses in integrity. The swearing (the kids started a "Coach Campbell Swore" fund, demanding ten bucks from Bill for every curse word; that fund became a down payment on the school's new football field). The way he listened intently to the kids and would take them aside for quick 1:1s. The tough talk, and sincere love. It didn't matter if you were a middle school kid or an exec at a big corporation: Bill's approach didn't waver.

The same thing worked for much more advanced football players, too. Charlie Batch grew up in Bill's hometown, Homestead, Pennsylvania, and they grew to be friends over the years, working together to help Homestead. Charlie played quarterback at Eastern Michigan University and then for fifteen years in the NFL for the Detroit Lions and Pittsburgh Steelers, who play their home games about ten miles from Homestead. In 2012, the starting quarterback for the Steelers, Ben Roethlisberger, got injured, and Charlie stepped in. Things didn't go well in that game: Charlie threw three interceptions and the Steelers lost to the Browns. The week after that loss, Bill and Charlie saw each other at an event in Homestead. Bill didn't do that finger-popping thing, but he might as well have. He had watched the game, and he chewed Charlie out pretty good, telling him to change his attitude, step up, take responsibility, and be a pro. Charlie was taken aback but not surprised. The coach was right.

The following Sunday, Charlie led the Steelers back from a ten-point deficit to beat their rivals, the Baltimore Ravens, and threw five completed passes on the winning drive. As he walked out of the victorious locker room he got a text from Bill: "Told you."

---

## WINNING RIGHT

### STRIVE TO WIN, BUT ALWAYS WIN RIGHT, WITH COMMITMENT, TEAMWORK, AND INTEGRITY.

---

## LEADERS LEAD

When Dan Rosensweig joined Chegg in 2010, he had been told they were six months away from an IPO. In fact, they were about three months away from bankruptcy. But he righted the ship and led it to an IPO in 2013, whereupon the stock tanked, dropping well below its IPO price. Dan, feeling the strain after a tough multiyear slog, was privately starting to lose faith. Was this company going to make it? Was he the right guy to lead it? He was thinking about quitting but didn't tell anyone.

Then he got a call from Bill, who had been coaching Dan for a few years, helping him through the ups and downs at Chegg.

"Dan," he said, "let's take a walk."

"Right now? Should I come over?"

"No, we're going to take a virtual walk, right here on the phone."

Uh-oh, Dan thought, looking past the mini football

helmets on his desk and out the window at the fountain in the courtyard below. "Where are we going?" he asked.

"Behind the woodshed," Bill replied.

He went on to lecture Dan about how he needed to stick with it at Chegg. Leaders lead, he told him. You can't afford to doubt. You need to commit. You can make mistakes, but you can't have one foot in and one foot out, because if you aren't fully committed then the people around you won't be, either. If you're in, be in.

"I don't know how he knew I was thinking of leaving," Dan says, "but he did. And he wasn't having it." Dan did not quit. He *led*. He rallied his team, which is still intact, and together they turned around and built the company.

It's great and fun to talk about winning, but what about losing? Bill knew something about losing. His teams at Columbia lost a lot, and the startup he joined, GO, failed, losing a lot of investor money in the process.* Failure is a good teacher, and Bill learned from these experiences that loyalty and commitment are easy when you are winning and much harder when you are losing. But that's, as Dan's story highlights, when loyalty, commitment, and integrity are even more important. When things are going badly, teams need even more of those characteristics from their leaders.

At Columbia, after a particularly tough loss, Bill yelled at his team in the locker room; he really read them the riot

---

* "Thank God for Webvan," Bill loved to say. "They lost so much money they made people forget about GO." Webvan raised more than $400 million from private investors and another $375 million from a 1999 IPO. It went bankrupt in 2001. GO lost about $75 million.

act. "That was the team I lost," he later said, "and that's the moment I lost them." He didn't rally the team, he didn't show them his loyalty, and he didn't make decisions that might help them. He just yelled at them. This was a moment he filed away. The moment he truly lost.

Decisiveness also becomes more important in challenging situations, as illustrated by the final days of GO. In *Startup*, Jerry Kaplan describes a pivotal moment that came one afternoon when Bill requested that the company's senior execs gather for an emergency meeting. The company had been struggling for a while, with virtually no sales and tough competition from Microsoft. Bill came to the conclusion that the company was not going to survive, much less be successful. He suggested to his team that they should sell the company, and after some discussion, they agreed. The reasoning, though, wasn't financial per se. They didn't want to sell to salvage at least some financial returns for themselves or for investors. They wanted to preserve the work they had done. "The important thing is to save the project and the organization—to protect what we've built," Bill said. He hoped to accomplish this by selling to a larger company that could fund and continue the work, even if that meant he'd be out of a job. In this case, Bill's loyalty wasn't to the company so much as to the cause.[10]

So, when you're losing, recommit to the cause. *Lead*. Nirav Tolia, currently CEO of Nextdoor, was the CEO of a dot-com startup called Epinions and a coachee of Bill's. Epinions went through several near-death experiences before eventually merging with a company called DealTime and relaunching as part of Shopping.com. When Nirav and the board decided to start looking for that merger, he informed his management team. One of the key team members, let's call him Bob, got spooked and within a few weeks left Epinions for a more stable situation. "That was a real body blow," Nirav says. "It was very traumatic that he left." Nirav got on the phone with Bill and told him about the departure. I'm coming over, Bill replied.

Nirav convened his team when Bill arrived at the office. Bill walked into the room. "I love you guys," he said. "There's something that's really bothering me. Bob leaving, he betrayed us. He was disloyal. He left us in our time of need. Fuck him." And that was pretty much it. Bill got up and walked out, not just out of the room but out of the building.

A few minutes later Nirav got a call, Bill again. "I bet no one else is going to quit on you now."

---

## LEADERS LEAD

WHEN THINGS ARE GOING BAD, TEAMS ARE LOOKING FOR EVEN MORE LOYALTY, COMMITMENT, AND DECISIVENESS FROM THEIR LEADERS.

---

# FILL THE GAPS BETWEEN PEOPLE

Eric was involved in a Google meeting, with some people attending in person in Mountain View, and some (including Eric) joining via videoconference. They were discussing a few different issues, but they ran out of time and one of the issues didn't get resolved. One person made a comment toward the end of the meeting, which Eric interpreted negatively. He felt sure, based on that one remark, that things weren't going to go his way on the issue in question. The comment sat with him and festered for a full week, and by the time the group got back together, Eric was gunning for battle. That is when he realized, though, that he had completely misunderstood the comment and, as a result, the entire situation. The crisis was inadvert. A lack of communication and an apparent slight had dug a fissure that was completely false.

This is not an unusual story. It happens every day: the offhand comment, the quickly drafted email or text, and people career off in emotional directions way out of whack with reality. This is when a coach can really come in handy. As Bill described it, his job as our coach was to "see little flaws in the organization that with a little massage we can make better. I listen, observe, and fill the communication and understanding gaps between people." The coach can spot those fissures before they become deep and permanent, and act to fix them by filling in the information gaps and correcting any miscommunication. Bill wasn't involved in that meeting with Eric, but if he had been, Eric would have gone to him to test out his assumptions about the perceived slight. Bill would have corrected him—everyone was, in fact, aligned—and Eric would have been spared a lot of angst.

So what would Bill do? First, he would listen and observe. This is the power of coaching in general: the ability to offer a different perspective, one unaffected by being "in the game." (Patrick Pichette: "Bill saw all the chess pieces all the time, because he had the luxury of not being on the board.") Bill sat in Eric's weekly staff meetings, listening intently, watching the body language of attendees, sensing mood shifts.

Marissa Mayer tells a story about Bill's power of observation. She had started a new program at Google for people right out of college, computer science majors who were brought into the company as "associate product managers." One day Eric told her, "Marissa, you've hired all the smartest twenty-three-year-olds on the planet. But they are driving everyone crazy. Either this becomes a home run or the whole thing blows up. Get them under control."

Marissa turned to Bill. Could he help? He agreed to attend one of their meetings, an evening session where the first class of APMs gave updates on their projects and what problems they were having. Marissa thought the meeting was a failure—it was so boring! Just a bunch of people giving status updates and griping.

Bill observed something different. After the meeting he took Marissa aside. They are all getting stuck, he said, and you are the wrong person to help them. You've been here since almost the beginning and know how to get things done, so you can't relate to the problems they are having. Get someone who will help them figure out what the next step is. Create a forum where they can help each other. That will fix the problem. And of course, he was right.

This is one example of the power of observation at work; listening, looking for patterns, assessing strengths and weaknesses. As Lee C. Bollinger says, "Bill had the highest capacity to understand the people he was working with. He had an intuitive sense of people and what motivated them and how to move them forward." He accomplished a lot of this by looking for tension, the smoke to a problem's fire. In Eric's staff meetings, for example, he'd sit in the room, usually not saying much, sensing when tension levels were rising and from where. Our staff meetings were generally open, transparent affairs where everyone was encouraged to share opinions and ideas, even on issues not directly related to their functions. Still, that goes only so far. People would simmer, and Bill would spot it.

This requires keen observation. Not just listening to the words, but noticing the body language and the side conversations. So many of the people we talked to commented on Bill's ability to sense when people were frustrated. This is a natural skill, but one that can be developed. You have to listen and watch.

Jim Rudgers, who was on Bill's coaching staff at Columbia, recalls Bill's remarkable ability to see the entire field of twenty-two players as a play unfolded. Hold up a finger and look at it, Jim says. That's how most of us watch football; the finger is the player with the ball. But Bill could see, recall, and assess the things that happen on the periphery as well. He brought that skill to team meetings. He wouldn't just see the speaker, he could see the entire field and gauge reactions and intents even with the people who remained silent, the ones without the ball.

Then he would talk to people. As Bill explained it one time at a Google management seminar: "I have a little more time than Larry does to do some of that stuff. I have a little more time than Sundar does to do some of that stuff, so, you know, I'll say to Sundar, Do you want me to meet with so-and-so? Sure. And here's what I'm going to tell 'em. You okay with that? Yeah. Great. Perfect, and, you know, that helps a little bit in moving the thing along. Let's get it moving."

Rachel Whetstone recalls a time a decision didn't go her way when she was running communications and policy for Google. She was in one of Eric's staff meetings, where they were discussing an important issue that had been causing PR headaches. She had been pushing for a change for a while, and when she didn't get the decision she wanted, she was upset. She felt they were making a mistake. Bill sought her out after the meeting. Listen, he told her, we decided not to make that change to that particular thing this time. I'm sorry and I know it's tough, but you're going to have to suck it up. Deal with the problem, okay?

Not much of a pep talk, right? His advice was "deal with it"! But sometimes that's all it takes. An acknowledgment that things didn't go your way, some empathy that it sucks, a reminder to buck up and soldier on for the team. These were the sort of messages that Bill delivered all the time. Short, timely, and highly effective.*[11]

---

\* Most research about delivering bad news shows that empathy is critical to doing it well. A 2000 paper for oncologists who have to bring bad news

And while the skill of observing tension is a challenging one to develop, this idea of going around and talking to people is not. It simply takes time, and the ability to communicate well with colleagues. Bill could have noted Rachel's frustration and simply forgotten about it; it wasn't his job to fix her problem. But instead he made the effort to have a conversation with her. To make that short, important connection. It's so easy to forget to have these little conversations in a busy day; Bill made it a priority.

While none of this was underhanded or secretive, it all had a behind-the-scenes quality. Bill rarely talked about these little 1:1 conversations; he would simply take you aside and have a few quiet words. This was all by design, another difference between a sports coach (who's out in front, leading the team, highly visible) and a business coach. As Deb Biondolillo says, Bill was "the shadow behind you. You hear him, but you are the one in front. He could be less confined, more genuine if he was in the background."

This was all done without an agenda. Bill often didn't voice an opinion about which way a decision would go—he just pushed for the decision to be made. When he sensed those moments, he'd work behind the scenes, drawing out people's points of view, closing communication gaps, and fixing miscommunications, so that when the time came to discuss things in the meeting and make the decision, everyone was prepared.

Then Bill would sit back, observe, and start the cycle over again.

---

to patients notes that until "the emotion is cleared" (through empathy), it's difficult to go on and discuss a plan.

# FILL THE GAPS BETWEEN PEOPLE

## LISTEN, OBSERVE, AND FILL THE COMMUNICATION AND UNDERSTANDING GAPS BETWEEN PEOPLE.

# PERMISSION TO BE EMPATHETIC

When you sum up the principles Bill used to build teams, and try to apply them as a manager, you give yourself, as Bradley Horowitz puts it, the "permission to be empathetic." After a successful career in the valley at Virage and Yahoo, Bradley co-led development of Google+, followed by its far more successful offspring, Google Photos. He met with Bill several times over this span and was always impressed by how he invariably led off the meetings by talking about personal stuff: What was going on with Bradley's family? What motivated him? Bill's approach was to make the human connection first, then approach the work with that understanding.

"This touchy-feely stuff isn't in the manual," Bradley says. "It's so easy to get wrapped up in the work of what we're producing, and not how we're doing it. But leading teams becomes a lot more joyful when you know and care about people. It's freeing." (One reason empathy isn't in the manual, according to *The Athena Doctrine*, a 2013 book by John Gerzema and Michael D'Antonio, is that it is typically seen as a feminine trait.[12] The proverbial manual was mostly written by men!)

Bradley got the chance to apply what he learned from Bill when he was tasked with figuring out what to do with Google+. The product had been launched with great fanfare as Google's entry into social networking. Google+ failed to get widespread adoption, but a few components, including its photo management features, were quite popular. So Bradley and other team members devised a plan to spin Photos off as a stand-alone product. They got buy-in from senior leadership and got to work.

The problem was, many of the engineers and product managers who had worked on Google+, including many senior people, had left the team and in many cases the company. Many of those who remained on the team had never led a project of this scope before. Bradley and the team knew there was a great product market fit—it was the right product for mobile users who loved photos (just about everyone!) at the right time. But was it the right team to deliver and were they set up to succeed?

Bradley put Bill's approach, the permission to be empathetic, to work. He prioritized his time to focus not on tactical and technical issues, but on team ones. He got to know and care about team members as people, pumped them up, pushed and implored them, then helped build momentum as they started to achieve important milestones. He focused on the team and not the problem, and the team responded.

Senior leads started stepping up as Bradley gave them more freedom.

At one point, as the project was really starting to roll, one of the most important technical leads on the team came to Bradley. He knew he was performing well, and he demanded more power and responsibility, which he was currently sharing with another lead. If not, he would go to Facebook, which had just given him a very nice offer.

It didn't take Bradley long to decide. The team that he had nurtured through empathy was more important than the one person. "I guess you're going to Facebook," he said.

---

## PERMISSION TO BE EMPATHETIC

### LEADING TEAMS BECOMES A LOT MORE JOYFUL, AND THE TEAMS MORE EFFECTIVE, WHEN YOU KNOW AND CARE ABOUT THE PEOPLE.

---

Bill Campbell employed all of these techniques, from hiring well (pick the right players) to promoting gender diversity (get to the table) to taking care of small misunderstandings before they become big (fill the gaps between people), to help teams achieve greatness. And the essence of Bill was the essence of just about any sports coach: team first. All players, from stars to scrubs, must be ready to place the needs of the team above the needs of the individual. Given that commitment, teams can accomplish great things. That's why, when faced with an issue, his first question wasn't about the issue itself, it was about the team tasked with tackling the issue. Get the team right and you'll get the issue right.

# CHAPTER 5

# The Power of Love

In February 2003, Brad Smith had just been hired as a new executive at Intuit. The hiring had entailed some drama, with a claim from one of Brad's former employers that by joining Intuit Brad had violated some noncompete agreements. It took some time, lawyering, and money to work things out. Not long after the dust settled and Brad joined the company, he attended an internal Intuit leadership conference, where the top people from all over the world gathered to discuss the company's plans and get to know each other better. It was a great opportunity for Brad to meet his new colleagues and make a strong first impression.

The first morning of the conference, as people filled coffee cups and caught up with friends and colleagues, Brad milled among them, exchanging handshakes and greetings.

Suddenly he was grabbed from behind and wrapped in a bear hug. Bill Campbell's first words to Brad: "So you're the son of a gun who cost me so much money. You better be worth it!" Except he used a more colorful term than "son of a gun."

We do not necessarily recommend that you greet new colleagues with hugs and curses. Personally, we still favor handshakes and more traditional conversational niceties. Everyone has their own style, obviously; hugs and curses was Bill's. What's more important is what it meant, to Bill and to the many of us on the receiving end. The reason Bill was able to get away with his hugs-and-curses approach was that all of his behavior was rooted in his heart: it came from love. "Get away" isn't the right way to describe it; people looked forward to Bill's hugs and profanities, because they meant he loved you.

Yes, love. Let's be clear: the kind of love we are referring to here is entirely chaste. He never crossed the line or came close to it. He hugged just about everyone, and if he couldn't get close enough to hug you, sometimes he'd blow kisses. Right there in the middle of a board meeting or Eric's staff meeting, Bill would give you a wink and blow you a kiss. Everyone understood with great clarity the intent of the hugs and kisses: to show that he cared, to show that he loved.

Academic studies point out that there is a "compensation effect" between warmth and competence: people tend to assume that people who are warm are incompetent and those who are cold, competent.[1] This of course was not the case with Bill; as Google cofounder Sergey Brin says, "He's that great combination of a sharp mind and a warm heart." But when Jerry Kaplan first met Bill at GO, he assumed he was just a "rough and tumble...middle-aged man."[2] Which means that you should lead with warmth, but know that you might have to work just a bit harder to build your reputation for competency.

Love is a word you don't hear a lot in business settings. Oh sure, maybe people will express love toward an idea, a product, a brand, or a plan. Or to that dessert they are serving in the cafeteria today. But not to a person. We've all been conditioned and trained to separate our personal emotions from the business environment. We all want to hire people with passion, but only in the business sense, of course, lest the lawyers and HR people get concerned. So what happens, what we live with daily, is an existence where our human selves and working selves are practically separate beings.

But not Bill. He didn't separate the human and working selves; he just treated everyone as a person: professional, personal, family, emotions . . . all the components wrapped up in one. And if you were one of his people, he cared about you fiercely and genuinely. "When Bill walked into the office at Benchmark, it was like a party arriving," Bill Gurley says. "He'd walk around greeting people by name, hugging them." After the hugs and greetings, he would talk about families, trips, friends. Bill was a coach of teams and a lover of people. What we learned from him is that you can't be one without the other. Academic research, as usual, bears this out, showing that an organization full of the type of "companionate love" that Bill demonstrated (caring, affectionate) will have higher employee satisfaction and teamwork, lower absenteeism, and better team performance.[3]

Earlier in the book we recount a story from Jesse Rogers,

about how when he launched his new company, Bill called him up and chewed him out about his crummy website. Jesse recalls that story through a combination of laughter and tears, then he notes something we heard a few times in our conversations about Bill. The ranting, the getting in his face over a crappy website, "came from a place of love," Jesse says. "The concept of male love is something people aren't used to talking about. When he is yelling at you, it's because he loves you and cares and wants you to succeed."

John Donahoe calls it, with appropriate reverence for Huey Lewis and the News, "the power of love." "He had a way of communicating that he loved you. And that gave him license to tell you that you are full of shit and you can do it better . . . It was never about him. Coming from him, it didn't hurt when he told you the truth."

So this is what we learned from Bill: that it's okay to love. That people in your team are people, that the whole team becomes stronger when you break down the walls between the professional and human personas and embrace the whole person with love.

Literally, in Bill's case.

## TOP TEN "BILLISMS"

Bill often had a unique way of telling you that he loved you. These are his top ten favorites, as recalled by his Columbia friend and teammate Ted Gregory. They were printed on the back page of the program given to guests at Bill's memorial service.

10. "You should have that shirt cleaned and burned."

9. "You're as dumb as a post."

8. "He's one of the great horse's asses of our time."

7. "You're a numbnuts."

6. "You couldn't run a five-flat forty-yard dash off a cliff."

5. "You've got hands like feet."

4. "You'd fuck up a free lunch."

3. "You're so fucked up you make *me* look good."

2. "Don't fuck it up."

1. "That's the sound of your head coming out of your ass."

## THE LOVELY RESET

"To care about people you have to care about people." This seems like it should be some hoary quote; we heard it a few times in our conversations with people about Bill. It's not, at least not one we can find anywhere online, so we will henceforth claim it. To care about people you have to care about people! You hear over and over again in corporate-speak that a company's most important asset is its people, that businesses put their people first, that they care about their employees, that blah blah blah. These aren't necessarily empty words; most companies and executives truly do care about their people. Perhaps just not the whole person.

Bill cared about people. He treated everyone with respect, he learned their names, he gave them a warm greeting. He cared about their families, and his actions in this regard spoke more loudly than his words. Jesse Rogers talks about how much his daughter cared for Bill, about how Bill always took the time, when he saw her, to give her a big hello hug. Ruth Porat says that when she took the job as Google's CFO and started commuting back and forth from New York, Bill's primary concern was how her husband was faring with the arrangement. Was he happy? What could Bill do to help out? "He cared about the whole you," Ruth says. "We talked about that a lot."

Sundar Pichai recalls that Bill would start every one of their weekly Monday meetings by asking about Sundar's family and weekend and talking about his own. "I was always busy going into these meetings, with lots of things to do, but my time with Bill always gave me a sense of perspective. That whatever I was doing was important, but he showed me that what really matters at the end of the day is how you live your life and the people in your life. It was always a lovely reset." Bill's small talk about families wasn't small at all. It provided his coachees a respite in a busy day and a chance to ease their work-family conflict at least momentarily.

Bill didn't reserve his care just for executives. When Mickey Drexler was on the Apple board and traveled to Cupertino for meetings, he often stopped in the local J.Crew store (he was J.Crew's CEO) at nearby Stanford Shopping Center. There the sales associates would often tell him about how his friend Bill had been shopping there. They loved Bill Campbell in that store. Bill learned the names of the salespeople, always greeted them warmly, and treated everyone with respect, as equals. "He acted the same way with the store associates as he did with the people on the Apple board," Mickey says. "I learned from that."

None of this feels that novel, does it? When we get together with colleagues, we often inquire about their families. The difference with Bill, and the hard thing to do in a busy business environment, is that he somehow found a way to *get to know* the families. Many times, he accomplished this simply by taking the questions a few steps beyond the "how are the kids?" norm. With Jonathan, it wasn't just how was the family, it was how did Hannah do at her latest soccer game? Which evolved into where was she thinking about college? Which evolved into some detailed advice about where she would fit best. Then, when he'd see the family at various events, they'd get the same hug as anyone else.

Bill developed this habit early in his career. Marc Mazur,

an advisor at Brightwood Capital, had known Bill since Coach Campbell recruited him to be a kicker at Columbia in the late 1970s. During the recruiting visit, Bill walked into the Mazur home and quickly surmised that it was a maternal one. I'll always take care of your son, Bill told Mrs. Mazur. The following year, as a freshman, Marc injured the knee of his kicking leg. He was not going to be kicking field goals for the Lions, not that season or any other. Bill called Marc's mom and told her that his promise held. He would still look after Marc, and he promised that Marc would not lose his financial aid if he couldn't play. Marc was on the freshman team at the time, and it was rare for the varsity coaches, much less the head coach, to get involved with the freshmen. But Bill did, and Marc and Bill were close for the rest of Bill's life, precisely because of the loyalty Bill showed Marc and his family.

Recruiting discussions like the ones Bill had with Marc's mother surely proved to Bill the importance of having a team member's family understand that the organization cares about the player, and vice versa. Nextdoor CEO Nirav Tolia was only twenty-six when he started working with Bill, and early in their relationship Bill asked for Nirav's father's phone number. After they talked, Nirav asked his father how the conversation with Bill went. "Fine," came the reply, but "Bill asked me not to share the details." Bill hadn't just asked Nirav about his family; he talked to them.

This wasn't the norm for Bill—once he left football, he didn't typically talk to people's parents. But there were plenty of instances when Bill cared about a person by caring about that person's family, not just by asking about their well-being but by actually caring about them. In some cases (including Eric's, who lost his father when he was twenty-six), Bill became a father figure to his mentees. Like Eric, Omid Kordestani lost his dad when he was young, and he came to see Bill as a father figure "who was full of heart and wisdom." When Omid took over as executive chairman of Twitter, he got together with Bill to talk about the role, given Bill's experience as chairman of Intuit, but they spent most of that time talking about family. Only after they covered the important stuff did they get to talking about Twitter.

And when the situation was more dire, Bill always made himself available to the families. When Mike Homer, a close friend and colleague of Bill's at Apple and GO, fell ill with Creutzfeldt-Jakob disease, Bill was a frequent visitor at his home and helped however he could, prioritizing Mike over his work at Google and other companies. He got to know Mike's caregivers by name, always chatting with them. "He wanted to let them know that Mike was well loved by family and friends," Mike's widow, Kristina Homer Armstrong, says. "He hoped that would encourage them to do their very best."

Similarly, when Steve Jobs became incapacitated by cancer, Bill visited him nearly every day, whether Steve was at home, in the office, or in the hospital. Phil Schiller, Apple's longtime head of marketing, worked with and was friends with both of them. He recalls, "Bill showed me that when you have a friend who is injured or ill or needs you in some way, you drop everything and just go. That's what you do, that's how you really show up. That's what Bill would do. Just go."

Caring and compassion can have a tremendous impact on an organization. When Bill was CEO of Intuit, one of his team leaders, Mari Baker, had a medical issue while traveling on a business trip and was hospitalized. When Bill got wind of the situation, he chartered a jet to fly Mari's husband to the East Coast to be with her and bring her home. At first blush, this seems like merely a generous gesture, but in fact stories like that can signal the devotion of the leader to the entire company and engender tremendous loyalty in return.[4]

Mark Human, who runs the El Dorado Golf and Beach Club in Cabo San Lucas, Mexico, tells a similar story about an employee of his. Bill had a vacation home at El Dorado and got to know Mark well during his years of vacationing there. Mark was a young manager, still in his twenties, when he met Bill, and today he recalls how Bill would always take the time to say hello, give him a hug, and whisper something positive in his ear. That stuck with Mark. "You have to take the time to smell the roses, and the roses are your people," he says. "Recognize that people want to talk to you about other things than just the job." Mark had one employee who was badly injured while helping out a family at the club. Mark helped rally a support group to get the young man the months of medical care that he needed; now he is completing his education and returning to work at the club.

Mark and his staff also take the time to make the annual year-end employee party a truly special occasion. People get dressed up, and no matter your level or background, you dance. Mark's turnover rate is low compared to the numerous other resorts in Cabo, which he attributes to the culture he helped create that was inspired by Bill.

Compassion isn't just good, it's good for business, and a 2004 paper argues that compassion at an individual level, such as what Bill and Mark demonstrated, can turn into "organizational compassion" when team members collectively notice, feel, and respond to pain experienced by team members. This happens when the organization "legitimates" that empathy, for example when leaders like Bill or Mark take the lead in helping individual team members. Compassion can start at the top.[5]

In our own lives, we don't try to match the way in which Bill loved people. We don't hug; we don't go quite as deep into people's family lives. We don't call their fathers! If you don't naturally have as big a heart as Bill's, faking it won't work. Repeat: don't fake it! But most of us like our coworkers. We care about them, but we check all but the most sanitized feelings at the door when we walk into the office. Bill taught us to do the opposite. Bring it in! Ask the questions about the family, learn people's names, then ask more questions, then look at the pictures, and, above all, care.

---

## THE LOVELY RESET

TO CARE ABOUT PEOPLE YOU
HAVE TO CARE ABOUT PEOPLE:
ASK ABOUT THEIR LIVES OUTSIDE
OF WORK, UNDERSTAND THEIR
FAMILIES, AND WHEN THINGS GET
ROUGH, SHOW UP.

---

# THE PERCUSSIVE CLAP

Imagine you are presenting a new product to the Apple board, sometime in the 2000s. Perhaps you are nervous as you walk into the room. There's Steve Jobs, there's Al Gore, and in between them sits Bill Campbell. You start talking about the product; maybe it's the new iPad or iPhone, maybe it's the latest Mac operating system. You talk about the timing, when the product will be released. Then you hold your breath and give the demo.

Sometime around then, the clapping starts. "Bill would clap and cheer, give double fist pumps, he would get so excited!" Phil Schiller recalls. "He provided an emotional reaction to the products, not a dry, boring, revenue-driven board reaction. He'd be out of his seat, an explosion of emotion." The effect of this wasn't so much about the approval of the product. It was about approval of the team. "It always felt like your uncle or dad just gave you appreciation and respect," Phil says. "That's one of the biggest things I learned from Bill. Don't just sit your butt in the seat. Get up and support the teams, show the *love* for the work they are doing."

"Everything Bill brought to the boardroom came from a place in his heart," says Bob Iger, CEO of Disney and an Apple board member. But there was another purpose behind the enthusiasm besides showing love for the team. "Once he started the applause," Bob says, "it was hard to disagree. The applause felt like it was coming from the board, not just Bill. It was his way of cheerleading, but also of moving things along." When Bob told us that, a little lightbulb went off. That was so Bill; of course that's what he was doing! With one gesture, a short outburst of enthusiastic clapping, he would both tell the team that he loved their work, giving them all a big pat on the back, *and* keep things moving. Bill's raucous cheerleading didn't just signal his approval, it generated momentum among the entire group in the room. What a brilliant technique!

Clay Bavor, the head of virtual and augmented reality products at Google, recalls a similar thing happening. In April 2015, Clay presented at a Google executive product review, showing off a new virtual reality headset and camera. After demoing the new gear, he passed out a low-end virtual reality viewer called Cardboard that Google had created and proceeded to walk everyone through a demo of a new app designed for the device. The program was called Expeditions; it let teachers take their classes on virtual tours of important sites around the world. Which meant that in this demo, Clay was the "teacher" and the executives were his "students." Clay felt a bit awkward, but suddenly, from the back of the room, came Bill's loud applause. "It was percussive," he says. "Like a gestural exclamation mark." Not a full round of applause, just five loud claps. "It really put me at ease. Like he was saying that what we did was cool, and it broke the ice for other people in the room to also get excited."

Today Clay has incorporated the "Bill Campbell clap"— the BCC—into the culture of the team. When someone announces something good in a meeting, someone else will erupt with five loud claps. If someone gives a burst of applause in the office, people will ask, "What was the BCC for?" Clay includes the BCC in training given to new team members; they even practice it in orientation. That team has hundreds of people now, every one of whom has learned Bill's percussive clap.

---

## THE PERCUSSIVE CLAP

### CHEER DEMONSTRABLY FOR
### PEOPLE AND THEIR SUCCESSES.

---

## ALWAYS BUILD COMMUNITIES

Super Bowl XIX was played in January 1985 at Stanford Stadium in Palo Alto, walking distance from Bill's home. The stadium was a large bowl, built in 1921 and lined with wooden benches renowned for leaving patrons with splinters as souvenirs of the day spent sitting and watching a game.[*] So when the Super Bowl came to town, Bill and the marketing team at Apple spied an opportunity: they lined the entire stadium, 80,000-plus seats, with cushions emblazoned with the Apple logo on one side and the Super Bowl's on the other. Since the game was practically in his backyard, and since he was personally responsible for saving the backsides of tens of thousands of fans, Bill decided to check it out for himself. He

---

[*] Including, in the late 1970s, a couple of local kids named Jonathan and Alan.

gathered a few of his buddies at his house, and together they walked to the stadium, picking up Steve Jobs en route. It was a great game on a cool, misty day. The 49ers beat the Miami Dolphins, and the guys all enjoyed themselves immensely.

This was the beginning of Bill's Super Bowl group, which rallied for the game every year. Bill would get the tickets and arrange transportation, while Columbia buddy Al Butts arranged hotels. The original group included Bill, Al, and their Columbia friends John Cirigliano and Ted Gregory. It grew to include, at times, Donna Dubinsky; Bill's brother Jim and his daughter Renee and her husband; Al's son Derek; Dave Kinser, his wife, Norma, and a rotating selection of their four kids; Spike Bloom (a friend from Kodak and Apple) and his son; Columbia buddy Gene Schatz; and Bill's kids Jim Campbell and Maggie Campbell and friends of theirs. They'd show up in the Super Bowl city on Thursday or Friday, find a good bar to make their temporary headquarters, and while away the time until kickoff, as Al says, "with lots of bad jokes, put-down exchanges, laughter, and the occasional deep conversation."

One year, when Bill had extra tickets, he gave them to a couple of incredulous kids whom he had spotted trying to buy cheap tickets from a scalper. When the sputtering scalper wondered why Bill had just given away something so valuable, Bill responded, "Because now the kids can enjoy themselves." Another year, when a couple of people had to cancel at the last minute, Bill invited the servers from the restaurant where the gang had dinner the night before to join them at the game. The women were delighted to accept!

"The Super Bowls were important to Bill," Al says. Not the game, but the group. "Bill's friends and their interactions with him and each other were enormously significant to him." When Bill passed away, he wanted to make sure that the tradition of the trip continued in his absence. So he endowed it. We've heard of people endowing scholarships, but a Super Bowl trip? That was Bill. He was so committed to ensuring this tradition continued that he left enough money to pay for it for at least another decade.

And that wasn't the only Bill trip. There was the annual baseball trip, which always included a Pirates game in Pittsburgh, a visit to Homestead, and a couple of other games in the Eastern time zone. There was the "yips and salsa" golf trip to Cabo San Lucas. There was the journey to the annual College Football Hall of Fame induction ceremony. There was the annual fishing trip to Butte, Montana, where Bill helped spearhead an annual charity event. All of these trips were endowed by Bill when he left us, so his friends could keep going even in his absence.

Back at Homestead, he sponsored the high school reunion, ensuring that his old gang could get back together on a regular basis. And even before he coached at Sacred Heart, he put together events after games where all the families could gather for a beer or a soda and a burger, to talk about the game and tell stories. Paying was never an option. Bill remembered his days as an assistant football coach at Boston College, when he noticed that some of the other coaches would sometimes skip social engagements, perhaps because they couldn't afford them. He wanted to make sure nobody skipped an event due to financial constraints, so he always picked up the tab.

The common thread with all these trips? Community. Bill built community instinctively. He knew that a place was much stronger when people were connected.

He cared so much about community that he invested in a place for people to gather. The Old Pro was a sports bar that opened in 1964 at the corner of El Camino Real and Page Mill Road in Palo Alto in a funky steel Quonset hut of unknown provenance. Bill started going there with his Intuit team in the 1990s, and when the bar was forced to move in the mid-2000s, he helped its owners Steve and Lisa Sinchek set up at a new, swankier location in downtown Palo Alto. Bill could be found there most every Friday afternoon, holding his own version of TGIF. Different people gathered there, always with plenty of food and beer, and when someone new showed up, Bill introduced him or her around with a generous spirit: he picked your best feature or accomplishment and highlighted it. The only rule was that you couldn't come there with an agenda. No one came to the Old Pro to "network" or to talk about deals. Bill liked the bar for its casual atmosphere, where formalities could drop by the wayside and people could just be themselves, whether laughing at old stories or talking business. It was the physical manifestation of the numerous communities he created. It is still one of the most popular spots in Palo Alto.

Bars seem to be a theme in Bill community-building stories. Phil Schiller tells the tale of the time Bill received an honorary degree from Boston College, where Bill had been assistant football coach before moving to the head job at Columbia. Phil is a BC grad and attended the ceremony. Afterward, Bill turned to Phil and suggested they head over to Mary Ann's, a well-known dive bar near campus. When they got there, Bill told the bartender that the Bud Lights (Bill's brew of choice) were on him that night, not just for their group but for the entire bar. It was graduation, so naturally the bar started filling up with proud parents and newly minted alums, most of whom were greeted with a cold one and a bear hug from an old football coach.

Community building has many similarities to the team-building practices we discuss in the previous chapter. To Bill, it was all part of a grand approach. Once you have your team or your community, what matters most are the bonds between the people on the team, which are forged by caring for each other and the common good. With all the trips Bill took with people, the trips were not the goal of the communities, the communities were the goal of the trips. It was all about making enduring connections between people, generating what sociologists call "social capital."[6] As John Cirigliano, a lifelong friend of Bill's dating back to their time at Columbia, says, "Bill fed off of the energy of people in his communities, the energy they generated as a result of being part of the community, and the same can be said for the people that he coached. In that way, he was a sort of perpetual motion machine."

Bill was fortunate enough to be able to afford a rather luxurious form of community building. Most people can't sponsor annual Super Bowl trips or buy a bar! But there are many ways to create social capital. Many of the people we talked to commented on Bill's penchant for connecting them to others; he was extraordinary at that. You would be talking to him about something and he would say, you should talk to so-and-so, I'll put you in touch. Minutes later the email would be on its way. He didn't do this randomly or for the sake of it; he made a quick calculation that the connection would be beneficial for both people. Which is a pretty good definition of community.

His get-togethers at the Old Pro are another example; for the cost of a few pitchers of beer, he gathered people on a weekly basis. Community building doesn't have to be expensive.

This principle may be easier to grasp in a social setting than a business one. Bill never talked to us about communities; he talked about teams. But we learned by observing his community activities. Invest in creating real, emotional bonds between people. Those are what endure and what make teams truly strong.

---

## ALWAYS BUILD COMMUNITIES

### BUILD COMMUNITIES INSIDE AND OUTSIDE OF WORK. A PLACE IS MUCH STRONGER WHEN PEOPLE ARE CONNECTED.

---

# HELP PEOPLE

Susan Wojcicki was an early employee at Google and spoke with Bill frequently over the years. A few years back, Susan, who was by then the head of YouTube, wanted to attend an important tech and media conference. Despite YouTube's status as one of the biggest video destinations for consumers around the world and an important player in the media and entertainment world, Susan could not secure an invitation. She worked through her considerable list of contacts, to no avail. In her 1:1 with Bill, she brought this up. He responded with a burst of colorful language. "This makes me so angry!" he said. "Of course you should be there!" They ended their meeting soon afterward, and a day later an invitation to the conference appeared in her inbox.

Bill did Susan a favor. He made a few calls and got her the invite. This is such a simple thing, but something surprisingly unusual in companies. We have had a couple of situations over the years where we asked colleagues to do us favors. These were not big favors, but they did entail bypassing processes or waiving minor rules. No one would have been hurt, and in fact the things we requested, if judged on merit alone, were absolutely the right things to do. Nevertheless, we were turned down. I'm sorry, I can't do that, was the generic response. You see, we've got this process in place . . .

To which Bill would have said: bullshit. Bill believed in doing favors for people. He was generous, he liked to help people, so when he could call on a friend to help the CEO of YouTube get into an event at which she absolutely belonged, he did it without hesitation. And it wasn't just fellow executives he helped. Bill got to know one of Jonathan's admins, a young woman named Chadé; they would chat on those rare occasions when Jonathan kept Bill waiting outside his office. One day Bill asked Chadé what she was up to, and she mentioned that she was considering studying for the LSAT and that she wanted to go to law school. Chadé was worried about how Jonathan would feel about the timing of her possible departure and struggling with when to apply and what and when to tell her boss.

When Bill saw Jonathan after meeting Chadé that day and told him about their conversation, Jonathan admitted that he didn't know his admin had her sights set on a number of top schools. "You should get to know your people better!" Bill told him. "Go out there and tell Chadé you'll survive no matter when she goes to school. And since you're her boss, make time and write her a recommendation. It's your job."

That next year, Chadé matriculated at Columbia Law School. She graduated a few years later and now practices law in Boston.

Bill enjoyed helping people and was incredibly generous. Good luck buying a dinner or a drink when Bill was around. One time, when he had a group of friends together in Cabo for vacation, Bill took all the kids to dinner; everyone got the bar T-shirt. He bought cases of very nice red wine to pour at his annual Christmas party, not because he enjoyed wine, but because he enjoyed watching his friends enjoy wine. You might think, well, heck, it's easy for a rich guy to buy everyone T-shirts and wine, and you'd be right. But Bill was that way well before he was rich. He had a generous spirit, which anyone can afford. For example, he was a very busy man, but he was generous with his time. Sometimes it took a couple of months to get on his calendar, but if you truly needed him, that phone call would come right away.

Most of the time, these little gifts were what Adam Grant, crediting businessman Adam Rifkin in his book *Give and Take*, calls "five-minute favors." They are easy for the person doing the favor, requiring minimal personal cost, but mean a lot to the recipient.[7] Grant also notes, in a 2017 article written with Reb Rebele, that "being an effective giver isn't about dropping everything every time for every person. It's about making sure that the benefits of helping others outweigh the costs to you." People who do this well are "self-protective givers." They are "generous, but they know their limits. Instead of saying yes to every request for help, they look for high-impact, low-cost ways of giving so that they can sustain their generosity—and enjoy it along the way."[8]

Helping people and being generous tie right back to the concepts of love and community we cover in this chapter. If your best friend asks you to do a favor, you do it, right? You love your friend, you trust her judgment (usually), you would do anything for her, so when she asks you to do something that would help her and is the right thing to do, there's no hesitation. But if she's your colleague at work, suddenly it's not so easy. You get those lines we heard: there's a process I have to go through, someone might somehow perceive that it's not fair, etc. So you don't do the favor.

We learned from Bill that it's okay to help people. Do favors. Apply judgment in making sure that they are the right thing to do, and ensure that everyone will be better off as a result. Then do the favor.

---

## HELP PEOPLE

## BE GENEROUS WITH YOUR TIME, CONNECTIONS, AND OTHER RESOURCES.

---

## LOVE THE FOUNDERS

One of the outcomes of Microsoft's failed attempt to buy Intuit was that Bill got to know a woman who at the time was the product manager on Microsoft Money, a product that competed with Intuit. Although the deal failed, she and Bill stayed in touch. She later left Microsoft and joined a Seattle startup called Amazon, and soon thereafter called up Bill and asked for an introduction to John Doerr. Bill made the introductions, and Kleiner Perkins ended up investing in Amazon.

A few years later, in 2000, Jeff Bezos, Amazon's founder and CEO, took some time off to spend time with his family. He had hired a COO, Joe Galli, but when he returned from his leave, the company was struggling. The board, which included Doerr and Scott Cook, was wondering if perhaps Jeff should step aside as CEO and elevate Joe to that role. Jeff would stay on as chairman and maybe have some other function. This had worked for Intuit when Bill replaced Scott as the CEO. But John and the others weren't sure. They asked Bill to spend some time in Seattle and report back.

Bill started traveling back and forth to the Pacific Northwest, going to the Amazon offices a couple of days per week, sitting in on management meetings and observing the company's operations and culture. After a few weeks, he reported back to the board that Jeff Bezos needed to stay as CEO. In his book about Amazon, *The Everything Store*, Brad Stone writes that "Campbell concluded Galli was unnaturally focused on issues of compensation and on perks like private planes, and he saw that employees were loyal to Bezos."[9]

Bill's recommendation came as a surprise to some board members, but his assessment carried the day and Jeff stayed as CEO, obviously with great success.

We have talked so far in this chapter about the love Bill had for people, and how it is so important for leaders to care about their people beyond the restrictive norms of the typical corporate environment. As long as we're on the topic, there's another type of love Bill prized: love of founders. He held a very special place in his heart for the people who have the guts and skills to start companies. They are sane enough to know that every day is a fight for survival against daunting odds and crazy enough to think they can succeed anyway. And retaining them in a meaningful way is essential to success in any company.

Too often we think about running a company as an operating job, and as we have already examined, Bill considered operational excellence to be very important. But when we reduce company leadership to its operational essence, we negate another very important component: vision. Many times operating people come in, and though they may run the company better, they lose the heart and soul of the company, the vision that is going to take it forward. This is where found-ers excel. Bill loved founders, not just for the chutzpah they possess to try entrepreneurship in the first place, but for the vision they have for the company, and the *love* they have for it. He understood their limitations, but he usually felt that their value outweighed the shortcomings.

Bill saw this scenario play out a few times. Perhaps the most spectacular example was at Apple. Bill was there when the new "business guy," John Sculley, came in as CEO, and he observed as Sculley eventually forced out cofounder Steve Jobs. Many years later, when Steve returned to Apple, he asked Bill to join the board to help him do what seemed im-possible: save the company, which was only a few months away from bankruptcy. Steve needed to change so much, to force the company to regain its singular focus on building superb products. He had to move fast, so he needed people he trusted to help him. Bill was at the top of that list. As they got to work, they became not just confidants but close friends. They took long walks together nearly every weekend, talking about Apple issues but also other things. Bill understood founders and understood why Steve was so exceptional. He supported Steve and was careful to protect him from the many who pursued him seeking one thing or another.

As Phil Schiller recalls, "They were like friends coming back together at a college reunion and trying to do one more thing together. Steve needed his help and strength to sup-port the plan. Sometimes he just needed an arm around the shoulder."

Bill was the business guy brought into GO, where founder Jerry Kaplan stayed on as a very important presence for the life of the company. Then he was the business guy who joined Intuit to replace Scott Cook as CEO. Again, Scott stayed on, to this day, as a very important presence. And Bill helped with perhaps the greatest and most challenging pairing of founders and incoming CEO, in coaching Eric, Larry, and Sergey at Google.

His principle every time: love the founders, and ensure they stay engaged in a meaningful way regardless of their operating role.

When Dick Costolo took over as CEO of Twitter, Bill counseled him to work well with the company's founders, Biz Stone, Jack Dorsey, and Evan Williams. Today you are the CEO and they are the founders, Bill said, but someday you will be the ex-CEO and they'll still be the founders. It's not you versus them; it's you and them. You are here to help them.

Many business leaders outside the startup world never have to grapple with the founder question, as the company's founder may be long gone by the time they join. Nevertheless, the essential argument in favor of founders remains: Vision is an important role. Heart and soul matter. Often that is embodied in the founder, but many other people may also embody what the company stands for, its mission and spirit. They don't show up on a balance sheet, income statement, or org chart, but they are very valuable.

---

## LOVE THE FOUNDERS

### HOLD A SPECIAL REVERENCE FOR—AND PROTECT—THE PEOPLE WITH THE MOST VISION AND PASSION FOR THE COMPANY.

---

# THE ELEVATOR CHAT

So many of the things we discuss in this chapter, indeed in this book, seem very personality dependent. Bill was perhaps the most "people person" we've ever met. So how does someone who isn't so naturally inclined to love people do it? Practice.

Bruce Chizen worked with Bill at Claris and later went on to become the CEO of Adobe Systems. When he first joined Adobe, in 1994, Bruce remembered what he had observed Bill do at Claris and tried to do the same. But it didn't come so naturally to him. "I tried to remember people's names," Bruce recalls. "When I ran into someone in the elevator, I'd start up a dialogue, how's it going, what are you working on? I would go out of my way to have lunch in the cafeteria with new people. I would put myself in interactions that were not as natural for me, but it made a difference."

Bruce attributes his success at Adobe in part to these more

social aspects of his work there. Before he ascended to the CEO spot, the company's founders asked him to take over products, something quite unusual for someone with a sales and marketing background. Their reasoning was that engineering leaders had developed a great deal of respect for him, due to his willingness to engage them and their developers in conversation.

The principles we outline in this book may not feel natural, but they can be learned. The key is pushing yourself to do it. When you're in that elevator, passing someone in the hallway, or seeing a group from your team in the cafeteria, take a moment to stop and chat. Bruce's lines are as good a starter as any: "How's it going? What are you working on?" In time, it becomes natural. "Trying to develop that personal connection didn't come that easily for me, but I worked at it," Bruce says. "Fortunately, it gets easier."

---

## THE ELEVATOR CHAT

### LOVING COLLEAGUES IN THE WORKPLACE MAY BE CHALLENGING, SO PRACTICE IT UNTIL IT BECOMES MORE NATURAL.

---

One of our big surprises in working on this book was how often the word *love* came up when people talked about Bill.

This isn't a typical word when speaking with tech executives, venture capitalists, and the like. But Bill made it okay to bring love to the workplace. He created a culture of what people who study these things call "companionate" love: feelings of affection, compassion, caring, and tenderness for others. He did this by genuinely caring about people and their lives outside of work, by being an enthusiastic cheerleader, by building communities, by doing favors and helping people whenever he could, and by keeping a special place in his heart for founders and entrepreneurs.

Love is part of what makes a great team great. Yes, this was a natural part of Bill's personality—he was way more ebullient than most of us! But it was also something he likely learned from football.

Steve Young, a Hall of Fame quarterback for the San Francisco 49ers, spoke of team love at a conference honoring Bill in September 2017. "Great coaches look beyond," Steve said. "[49ers coach Bill Walsh] would get the team together every year and say, 'Hey, guys, we're going to integrate this team.' There were all these little cliques—the safeties hang together, guys from different schools, socioeconomic backgrounds, geography, language, religion. He says, 'I'm going to break all of those . . .'

"He wanted us to get integrated with each other so when you're at Lambeau Field, down by four, with a minute and a half left and it's third-and-ten, it's sleeting, you're soaking wet and the wind is blowing and eighty thousand people are screaming at you. Human nature is saying get me out of here, I just want to get to the bus, get this over with.

"Now you're in the huddle and it's that moment. Everyone

looks at each other and it's like, we are integrated, we have a reason, we have a depth, we have a love for each other, a respect . . .

"Why did the 49ers do so great from 1981 to 1998? It's because we had a love for each other."*

---

* The 49ers reached the playoffs sixteen times in those eighteen seasons. Lambeau Field is the home stadium of the Green Bay Packers, a frequent 49er rival.

# CHAPTER 6

---

# The Yardstick

Eric decided to step down as Alphabet's executive chairman in December 2017, right around the time we were completing the first draft of this book. The timing was right. The company had successfully navigated a tricky transition from being just Google to being Alphabet, a holding company that oversees Google as well as a handful of burgeoning "other bets," such as Verily (life sciences) and Waymo (transportation). A new generation of leaders, including CEO Sundar Pichai, had taken the helm at Google and the company was thriving. It had successfully made the transition to a mobile-first, and, in many places, mobile-only, world and had a pipeline brimming with innovative products and services, driven by exciting breakthroughs in machine learning technologies.

Eric had been with Google for nearly seventeen years. He became chairman of the board in March 2001. Then he joined full-time as CEO in August 2001 and moved from CEO to executive chairman in April 2011. Now his full-time engagement with the company was coming to an end. He was considered by any measure to be an accomplished, successful person. And yet, as he discovered, just like anyone who is faced by a challenge or change, he needed emotional support.

When Eric became Google's CEO and when he moved to executive chairman, Bill Campbell was there to smooth the transitions. Bill talked to the individuals involved and made sure that the human, emotional side of things was being addressed. When the board asked Eric to step down as chairman before the IPO, Bill was there to talk him through it. As a result, when these changes were made, they weren't just transactions—they ended up *feeling* right. This time, there was no Bill. The entire process felt different. There was general agreement on the next steps, but there was no one there to guide Eric through the process. The team got to the best outcome for all, but the process was more businesslike, lacking the love and affirmation that Bill would have added.

Mentorship and coaching are intensely personal. Eric knew *what* Bill would have been telling him, and he knew what to do, but he badly missed *hearing* him say it.

This may all seem somewhat silly to an outsider. After all, this was a change among powerful, successful executives, operating with lofty titles—CEO, executive chairman—that the vast majority of people will never hold. What could Eric, or anyone else in this rarefied realm, possibly have to worry about? Why does an Eric Schmidt need *emotional support*?

In fact, it is often the highest-performing people who feel the most alone. They usually have more interdependent relationships but feel more independent and separate from others.[*][1] Their powerful egos and confidence help drive their success but may be paired with insecurities and uncertainty. They often have people who want to be their friends for personal gain rather than for friendship. They're human. They still need affirmation and to know they are appreciated. And when a human is stepping back from a place that has been part of his heart and soul for seventeen years, a place he helped to nurture and grow into something spectacular, a place he loves, he just might need a pat on the back, a big hug, and the assurance that everything is going to be okay, that there is a very exciting future out there. Which Bill was not there to deliver.

When we started the process of writing this book, we knew all about our own firsthand experiences of working with Bill, we knew how important he was to the success of Google, and we knew that he had worked with many other people throughout the valley. Through interviews with the people who knew and were coached by Bill, and through research into some of his principles, we learned so much more. A more detailed and complex model of his approach to management emerged, and we developed a thesis as to how critical his principles are to business success.

---

\* A 2001 paper by Fiona Lee and Larissa Z. Tiedens examines how these factors of interdependence and independence reinforce each other and notes that "power creates a subjective sense of separation and distinctiveness from others."

To be successful, companies need to have teams that work together as communities, where individuals integrate their interests and put aside differences to be individually and collectively obsessed with what's good and right for the company. Since this doesn't naturally happen among groups of people, especially high-performing, ambitious people, you need someone playing the role of a coach, a *team coach*, to make it happen. Any company that wants to succeed in a time where technology has suffused every industry and most aspects of consumer life, where speed and innovation are paramount, must have team coaching as part of its culture. This is especially true at its top levels; executive teams must have a coach if they want to perform at their best.

We were lucky to have a Bill Campbell acting as our team coach, but most teams aren't so lucky, which is fine. Because the best person to be the team's coach is the team's manager. Being a good coach is essential to being a good manager and leader. Coaching is no longer a specialty; you cannot be a good manager without being a good coach. The path to success in a fast-moving, highly competitive, technology-driven business world is to form high-performing teams and give them the resources and freedom to do great things. And an essential component of high-performing teams is a leader who is both a savvy manager and a caring coach.

In this book, we have explored how Bill approached his role as a coach of teams. He insisted on management excellence and hammered home the importance of simple practices that add up to a strong operation. He believed that managers who put their people first and run a strong operation are held as leaders by their employees; these managers don't assume leadership, they earn it. He had a thoughtful and consistent approach to communications. He prized decisiveness; strong managers recognize when the time for debate is over and make a decision. He appreciated "aberrant geniuses," those strong performers whose behavior can stray outside the norm, but also advocated moving on quickly if their behavior endangers the team. He believed that great products and the teams that create them are at the core of a great company. Everything else should be in service to that core. He knew that sometimes managers need to let people go, but they should also allow them to leave with their dignity intact.

He understood that relationships are built on trust, so he prioritized building trust and loyalty with the people he worked with. He listened completely, was relentlessly candid, and believed in his people more than they believed in themselves. He thought that the team was paramount, insisted on team-first behavior, and when faced with any issue his first step was to look at the team, not the problem. He sought out the biggest problems, the elephants in the room, and brought them front and center, ensuring they got looked at first. He worked behind the scenes, in hallway meetings, phone calls, and 1:1s, to fill communication gaps. He pushed leaders to lead, especially when things were bleak. He believed in diversity and in being completely yourself in the workplace.

He loved people. He brought that love to communities he created or joined. He made it okay to bring it into the workplace.

So we interviewed a bunch of people, we built a thesis, we enumerated Bill's principles and supported them with quotes and stories. But we hadn't really *felt* any of this until one of us, Eric, was faced with a major transition, and his coach wasn't there to help.

Jonathan was walking his dog Bo with his wife, Beryl, on a December afternoon in 2017. He had gotten the email from Eric that morning letting him know that Eric was stepping down. While the news was disconcerting to Jonathan, he could sense that Eric's uncertainty was even greater. He brought this up to Beryl. You have to help him, Beryl urged. Bo wagged in agreement.

Which made Jonathan wonder: If Bill were here, what would he do?

The answer was, Bill would have helped Eric figure out the best next steps for him. He would not have told Eric what to do; he would have helped him devise his own plan. He would have given him a hug and a pat on the back and reminded him just how great a job he had done at Google over the past seventeen years. He would have rallied a small community to surround Eric with the things he likes most—big ideas, new momentum, fascinating science, advanced technology. He would have done this with love and affirmation.

So that's what Jonathan started to do. He spoke with Eric and with Jared Cohen, who runs Alphabet's Jigsaw subsidiary and is a close friend of Eric's. He brought in Alan Eagle, and they started to put together ideas and a plan for a project they eventually called "Eric 3.0." But mostly, he cared and rallied others who cared to help out. Because through the journey of writing this book, the three of us have come to realize an essential truth about team coaching and how Bill did it.

Bill grasped that there are things we all care about as people—love, family, money, attention, power, meaning, purpose—that are factors in any business situation. That to create effective teams, you need to understand and pay attention to these human values. They are part of who we all are, regardless of our age, level, or status. Bill would get to know people as people, and by doing so he could motivate them to perform as businesspeople. He understood that positive human values generate positive business outcomes. This is a connection that too many business leaders ignore. Which is why we think it is so important that we all learn to do it now. It is counterintuitive in the business world, but essential to success.

Our small team gradually developed a plan for Eric's next stage in his career. That there is a plan is important. That there is a team is paramount.

# THE WHAT NEXT? DECISION

John Donahoe faced a situation somewhat similar to Eric's when he stepped down as CEO of eBay in 2015: successful businessman, past age fifty, kids grown . . . What do you do next? John tackled this question by interviewing dozens of people who were older than him but had retained plenty of vitality, asking them how they had approached similar transitions and how they stayed engaged in their later-in-life careers. The answers:

**BE CREATIVE.** Your post-fifty years should be your most creative time. You have wisdom of experience and freedom to apply it where you want. Avoid metaphors such as you are on the "back nine." This denigrates the impact you can have.

**DON'T BE A DILETTANTE.** Don't just do a portfolio of things. Whatever you get involved with, have accountability and consequence. Drive it.

**FIND PEOPLE WHO HAVE VITALITY.** Surround yourself with them; engage with them. Often they will be younger.

**APPLY YOUR GIFTS.** Figure out what you are uniquely good at, what sets you apart. And understand the things inside you that give you a sense of purpose. Then apply them.

**DON'T WASTE TIME WORRYING ABOUT THE FUTURE.** Allow serendipity to play a role. Most of the turning points in life cannot be predicted or controlled.

Bill usually did not take compensation for his work as a coach. When he first showed up at Dan Rosensweig's office, he told Dan, "I don't take cash, I don't take stock, and I don't take shit." He repeatedly declined offers of compensation for his work at Google, and when he finally accepted some stock, he donated it all to charity. This is not normal; most advisors to companies get paid in stock or cash. But Bill felt he had been amply compensated throughout his business career, and now he wanted to give back. As he told Ron Johnson, CEO of Enjoy, after Ron had stepped down from his CEO job at JCPenney in 2013, "If you've been blessed, be a blessing." Bill was a blessing.

When asked about his habit of eschewing compensation, Bill would say that he had a different way of measuring his impact, his own kind of yardstick. I look at all the people who've worked for me or who I've helped in some way, he would say, and I count up how many are great leaders now. That's how I measure success.

We interviewed more than eighty great leaders in working on this book, all of whom credit Bill with playing a major role in their success, and there are more we missed. Bill's yardstick is looking pretty good.

We hope that in reading this book you have picked up some principles on how to be a better manager and coach. We hope that you are thinking about how to make your team great, and how you can propel yourself to be great, to go beyond your self-imposed limits. We hope that you will become another leader on Bill's yardstick. Because the world faces many challenges, and they can only be solved by teams. Those teams need coaches.

# Acknowledgments

In writing this book, we have been entrusted with an important legacy, and for that we have to first and foremost thank Bill's widow, Eileen Bocci, and his children, Jim Campbell and Maggie Campbell. It was an honor and a pleasure to be given this tremendous opportunity.

We spoke with more than eighty people whose lives have been touched by Bill. All of them are busy, accomplished people. All of them gave us their time freely, and every one of them concluded our conversation with an offer to help in any way they could with the creation of this book. Thank you, all of you:

| | | |
|---|---|---|
| David Agus | Chase Beeler | Todd Bradley |
| Shellye Archambeau | Deborah Biondolillo | Sergey Brin |
| Kristina Homer Armstrong | Lee Black | Shona Brown |
| | Laszlo Bock | Eve Burton |
| Clay Bavor | Lee C. Bollinger | Al Butts |

| | | |
|---|---|---|
| Derek Butts | Bradley Horowitz | Patrick Pichette |
| Bruce Chizen | Mark Human | Peter Pilling |
| Jared Cohen | Chad Hurley | Ruth Porat |
| Scott Cook | Jim Husson | Jeff Reynolds |
| Dick Costolo | Bob Iger | Jesse Rogers |
| Eddy Cue | Eric Johnson | Dan Rosensweig |
| John Doerr | Andrea Jung | Wayne Rosing |
| John Donahoe | Salar Kamangar | Jim Rudgers |
| Mickey Drexler | Vinod Khosla | Sheryl Sandberg |
| David Drummond | Dave Kinser | Philip Schiller |
| Donna Dubinsky | Omid Kordestani | Philipp Schindler |
| Joe Ducar | Scotty Kramer | Chadé Severin |
| Brad Ehikian | Adam Lashinsky | Danny Shader |
| Alan Eustace | Ronnie Lott | Ram Shriram |
| Bruno Fortozo | Marissa Mayer | Brad Smith |
| Pat Gallagher | Marc Mazur | Esta Stecher |
| Dean Gilbert | Mike McCue | Dr. Ron Sugar |
| Alan Gleicher | Mary Meeker | Stacy Sullivan |
| Al Gore | Shishir Mehrotra | Nirav Tolia |
| Diane Greene | Emil Michael | Rachel Whetstone |
| Bill Gurley | Michael Moe | Susan Wojcicki |
| John Hennessy | Larry Page | |
| Ben Horowitz | Sundar Pichai | |

Like any important project, this was a team effort, and ours has been fantastic. Lauren LeBeouf kept us organized and managed all of those interviews, but more important, proved to be an astute and sensitive editor. She made this book much better.

Marina Krakovsky helped us connect Bill's principles with

academic research, showing that he was truly ahead of his time in the business management world. She is always creative and insightful, and a heck of an editor to boot. It was a great pleasure to work with you again, Marina!

Jim Levine is our constant agent, cheerleader, and coach, and guided us to the best title after much debate. Hollis Heimbouch pushed us in the right direction, edited us into elegance, and gently helped these sometimes clueless West Coast techies understand the world of publishing. Thank you both for your unflagging support and help!

Melissa Carson Thomas keeps our facts straight. She has an incredible eye for detail and a knack and passion for getting to the truth. Thank you for that, Melissa.

Marc Ellenbogen, Corey duBrowa, Winnie King, and Tom Oliveri are Google colleagues and friends who helped us navigate the ins and outs of big company legal and PR stuff while keeping the heart and soul of our tale intact.

Karen May oversees leadership training at Google and worked closely with Bill to help him teach his principles to Googlers. She helped us launch this project and provided several insightful additions to the manuscript.

Guy Kawasaki has written more than a dozen very successful books. He took the time to read ours and give us some very pointed, spot-on feedback! ("Do you guys really think this is almost finished?")

Adam Grant not only agreed to our request to write our foreword, but he supplied many interesting academic references, entertained us with a lengthy email tangent on sports teams, and provided a fantastic Charles Darwin quote.

Jennifer Aaker gave us plenty of feedback on narrative and

storytelling, which she teaches at Stanford's business school, but failed to make our book as funny as her family's travelogues.

Emmett Kim, Cindy Mai, and Andy Berndt got us rolling with some cover design concepts. Then Rodrigo Corral and Anna Kassoway took us the rest of the way, bringing a sometimes messy (and contentious) process to a beautiful conclusion. Thank you all for your patience and insane creativity.

Miles Johnson somehow parlayed his day job as a Google brand strategist into a decidedly less glamorous gig overseeing the creation of our website. It looks great, Miles!

Mindy Matthews is a brilliant copyeditor, keeper of tenses, slayer of extraneous, commas. The only sentences in this book that she didn't scrutinize with a picky eye for detail are these two.

Josh Rosenberg provided the most detailed edits of anyone who doesn't have the word *editor* in his job description. Although he's still mad we left the Warriors off the list of the all-time greatest sports dynasties. Hannah Rosenberg and Beryl Grace critiqued the work at every step and help remind Jonathan of Bill by regularly asking at the dinner table, "What would Bill do?"

Joanne Eagle was occasionally Alan and Jonathan's substitute English teacher in high school and apparently still feels like she has to mark up our papers. Thank you, Mom!

Mark Fallon is our Homestead connection, giving us invaluable info about Bill's hometown and an amazing portrait of Bill that hangs in Jonathan's office. It is literally infused with sand from Google's volleyball court.

Debbie Brookfield is Bill's longtime assistant who always greeted us so warmly when we trekked to Bill's office. She was the glue that held Bill's professional life together.

Ken Auletta talked several times with Bill about writing a book about him and gave us some great feedback on the manuscript. We're honored by his help.

Glenn Yeffeth, a good friend, is the successful publisher of BenBellaBooks and helped educate us with an insider's perspective on the publishing industry.

Josh and Jason Malkofsky-Berger take pride in being card-carrying members of the Jonathan fan club and choose to read and critique almost everything he writes.

Don Hutchison asks for early opportunities to read everything, so he can be the first to produce an excellent and highly ranked book review. Hurry up, Don!

Prem Ramaswami, our longtime collaborator at Google, always gives us great input and then incorporates only the best points in his college lectures.

Susan Feigenbaum taught Jonathan everything he knows about statistics in college, but also always gave him excellent insights on storytelling and narrative as well.

Matt Pyken—a real Hollywood writer!—suggested ways to add flair and keep our readers' eyes glued to every page.

Jeff Huang teaches philosophy and focuses on ethics and moral issues. He encouraged us to write a book about Bill so he could teach those principles in the classroom.

James Isaacs, Jonathan's former boss at Apple, is a lifelong learner himself and constantly pushes us to do better.

Dave Deeds, a professor of entrepreneurship, helped us

steer the manuscript to be accessible to all the founders and leaders of small companies, who spawn the majority of economic growth.

Eric Braverman, Cassie Crockett, and Dennis Woodside all took the time out of their busy schedules to read the manuscript and give us their thoughts. And Eric's and Cassie's "conceptual questions" still have us thinking.

Zach Gleicher is a Google product manager whom we met through Bill. Bill promised us that Zach would do a terrific job at Google. Bill never broke a promise!

# Notes

## Chapter 1: The Caddie and the CEO

1. Arthur Daley, "Sports of the Times; Pride of the Lions," *New York Times*, November 22, 1961.

2. "300 Attend Testimonial for Columbia's Eleven," *New York Times*, December 20, 1961.

3. Photograph courtesy of Columbia University Athletics.

4. Photograph courtesy of Columbia University Athletics.

5. George Vecsey, "From Morningside Heights to Silicon Valley," *New York Times*, September 5, 2009.

6. Charles Butler, "The Coach of Silicon Valley," *Columbia College Today*, May 2005.

7. P. Frost, J. E. Dutton, S. Maitlis, J. Lilius, J. Kanov, and M. Worline, "Seeing Organizations Differently: Three Lenses on Compassion," in *The SAGE Handbook of Organization Studies*, 2nd ed., eds. S. Clegg, C. Hardy, T. Lawrence, and W. Nord (London: Sage Publications, 2006), 843–66.

8. Butler, "The Coach of Silicon Valley."

9. Michael Hiltzik, "A Reminder That Apple's '1984' Ad Is the Only Great Super Bowl Commercial Ever—and It's Now 33 Years Old," *Los Angeles Times*, January 31, 2017.

10. Michael P. Leiter and Christina Maslach, "Areas of Worklife: A Structured Approach to Organizational Predictors of Job Burnout," *Research in Occupational Stress and Well Being* (January 2004), 3:91–134.

11. On the negative effects of power struggles, see L. L. Greer, Lisanne Van Bunderen, and Siyu Yu, "The Dysfunctions of Power in Teams: A Review and Emergent Conflict Perspective," *Research in Organizational Behavior* 37 (2017): 103–24.

On how status conflicts hurt teams: Corinne Bendersky and Nicholas A. Hays, "Status Conflict in Groups," *Organization Science* 23, no. 2 (March 2012): 323–40.

12. D. S. Wilson, E. Ostrom, and M. E. Cox, "Generalizing the Core Design Principles for the Efficacy of Groups," *Journal of Economic Behavior & Organization* 90, Supplement (June 2013): S21–S32.

13. Nathanael J. Fast, Ethan R. Burris, and Caroline A. Bartel, "Insecure Managers Don't Want Your Suggestions," *Harvard Business Review,* November 24, 2014.

14. Saul W. Brown and Anthony M. Grant, "From GROW to GROUP: Theoretical Issues and a Practical Model for Group Coaching in Organisations," *Coaching: An International Journal of Theory, Research and Practice* 3, no. 1 (2010): 30–45.

15. Steven Graham, John Wedman, and Barbara Garvin-Kester, "Manager Coaching Skills: What Makes a Good Coach," *Performance Improvement Quarterly* 7, no. 2 (1994): 81–94.

16. Richard K. Ladyshewsky, "The Manager as Coach as a Driver of Organizational Development," *Leadership & Organization Development Journal* 31, no. 4 (2010): 292–306.

## Chapter 2: Your Title Makes You a Manager. Your People Make You a Leader.

1. Fariborz Damanpour, "Organizational Innovation: A Meta-Analysis of Effects of Determinants and Moderators," *Academy of Management Journal* 34, no. 3 (September 1991): 555–90; Brian Uzzi and Jarrett Spiro, "Collaboration and Creativity: The Small World Problem," *American Journal of Sociology* 111, no. 2 (September 2005): 447–504.

2. Nicholas Bloom, Erik Brynjolfsson, Lucia Foster, Ron S. Jarmin, Megha Patnaik, Itay Saporta-Eksten, and John Van Reenen, "What Drives Differences in Management," Centre for Economic Performance Research discussion paper, No. DP11995 (April 2017).

3. Ethan Mollick, "People and Process, Suits and Innovators: The Role of Individuals in Firm Performance," *Strategic Management Journal* 33, no. 9 (January 2012): 1001–15.

4. Linda A. Hill, "Becoming the Boss," *Harvard Business Review*, January 2007.

5. Mark Van Vugt, Sarah F. Jepson, Claire M. Hart, and David De Cremer, "Autocratic Leadership in Social Dilemmas: A Threat to Group Stability," *Journal of Experimental Social Psychology* 40, no. 1 (January 2004), 1–13.

6. Nicholas Carlson, "The 10 Most Terrible Tyrants of Tech," Gawker. August 12, 2008, http://gawker.com/5033422/the-10-most-terrible-ty rants-of-tech.

7. Jeffrey Pfeffer and John F. Veiga, "Putting People First for Organizational Success," *Academy of Management Executive* 13, no. 12 (May 1999): 37–48.

8. Steven Postrel, "Islands of Shared Knowledge: Specialization and Mutual Understanding in Problem-Solving Teams," *Organization Science* 13, no. 3 (May 2002): 303–20.

9. Jerry Kaplan, *Startup: A Silicon Valley Adventure* (New York: Houghton Mifflin Harcourt, 1994), 198.

10. Joseph A. Allen and Steven G. Rogelberg, "Manager-Led Group Meetings: A Context for Promoting Employee Engagement," *Group & Organization Management* 38, no. 5 (September 2013): 543–69.

11. Jennifer L. Geimer, Desmond J. Leach, Justin A. DeSimone, Steven G. Rogelberg, and Peter B. Warr, "Meetings at Work: Perceived Effectiveness and Recommended Improvements," *Journal of Business Research* 68, no. 9 (September 2015): 2015–26.

12. Matthias R. Mehl, Simine Vazire, Shannon E. Hollenen, and C. Shelby Clark, "Eavesdropping on Happiness: Well-being Is Related to Having Less Small Talk and More Substantive Conversations," *Psychological Science* 21, no. 4 (April 2010): 539–41.

13. A deeper look at empowering opposing parties in mediation can be found in this article: Robert A. Baruch Bush, "Efficiency and Protection, or Empowerment and Recognition?: The Mediator's Role and Ethical Standards in Mediation," *University of Florida Law Review* 41, no. 253 (1989).

14. Kristin J. Behfar, Randall S. Peterson, Elizabeth A. Mannix, and William M. K. Trochim, "The Critical Role of Conflict Resolution in Teams: A Close Look at the Links Between Conflict Type, Conflict Management Strategies, and Team Outcomes," *Journal of Applied Psychology* 93, no. 1 (2008): 170–88.

15. James K. Esser, "Alive and Well After 25 Years: A Review of Groupthink Research," *Organizational Behavior and Human Decision Processes* 73, nos. 2–3 (March 1998): 116–41.

16. Ming-Hong Tsai and Corinne Bendersky, "The Pursuit of Information Sharing: Expressing Task Conflicts as Debates vs. Disagreements Increases Perceived Receptivity to Dissenting Opinions in Groups," *Organization Science* 27, no. 1 (January 2016): 141–56.

17. Manfred F. R. Kets de Vries, "How to Manage a Narcissist," *Harvard Business Review*, May 10, 2017.

18. Amy B. Brunell, William A. Gentry, W. Keith Campbell, Brian J. Hoffman, Karl W. Kuhnert, and Kenneth G. DeMarree, "Leader Emergence: The Case of the Narcissistic Leader," *Personality and Social Psychology Bulletin* 34, no. 12 (October 2008): 1663–76.

19. Henry C. Lucas, *The Search for Survival: Lessons from Disruptive Technologies* (New York: ABC-CLIO, 2012), 16.

20. Thomas Wedell-Wedellsborg, "Are You Solving the Right Problems?," *Harvard Business Review*, January–February 2017.

21. Manuela Richter, Cornelius J. König, Marlene Geiger, Svenja Schieren, Jan Lothschütz, and Yannik Zobel, "'Just a Little Respect': Effects of a Layoff Agent's Actions on Employees' Reactions to a Dismissal Notification Meeting," *Journal of Business Ethics* (October 2016): 1–21.

22. Ben Horowitz, *Hard Thing About Hard Things* (New York: Harper Business, 2014), 79.

23. Benjamin E. Hermalin and Michael S. Weisbach, "Board of Directors as an Endogenously Determined Institution: A Survey of the Economic Literature," *FRBNY Economic Policy Review* 9, no. 1 (April 2003): 7–26.

24. Jeffrey A. Sonnenfeld, "What Makes Great Boards Great," *Harvard Business Review*, September 2002.

### Chapter 3: Build an Envelope of Trust

1. Denise M. Rousseau, Sim B. Sitkin, Ronald S. Burt, and Colin Camerer, "Not So Different After All: A Cross-Discipline View of Trust," *Academy of Management Review* 23, no. 3 (1998): 393–404.

2. Tony L. Simons and Randall S. Peterson, "Task Conflict and Relationship Conflict in Top Management Teams: The Pivotal Role of Intragroup Trust," *Journal of Applied Psychology* 85, no. 1 (February 2000): 102–11.

3. Alan M. Webber, "Red Auerbach on Management," *Harvard Business Review,* March 1987.

4. Amy Edmondson, "Psychological Safety and Learning Behavior in Work Teams," *Administrative Science Quarterly* 44, no. 2 (June 1999): 350–83.

5. Suzanne J. Peterson, Benjamin M. Galvin, and Donald Lange, "CEO Servant Leadership: Exploring Executive Characteristics and Firm Performance," *Personnel Psychology* 65, no. 3 (August 2012): 565–96.

6. Carl Rogers and Richard E. Farson, *Active Listening* (Chicago: University of Chicago Industrial Relations Center, 1957).

7. Andy Serwer, "Gamechangers: Legendary Basketball Coach John Wooden and Starbucks' Howard Schultz Talk About a Common Interest: Leadership," *Fortune*, August 11, 2008.

8. Jack Zenger and Joseph Folkman, "What Great Listeners Actually Do," *Harvard Business Review,* July 14, 2016.

9. Kaplan, *Startup*, 199–200.

10. Mats Alvesson and Stefan Sveningsson, "Managers Doing Leadership: The Extra-Ordinarization of the Mundane," *Human Relations* 56, no. 12 (December 2003): 1435–59.

11. Niels Van Quaquebeke and Will Felps, "Respectful Inquiry: A Motivational Account of Leading Through Asking Questions and Listening," *Academy of Management Review* 43, no. 1 (July 2016): 5–27.

12. Ron Carucci, "How to Use Radical Candor to Drive Great Results," *Forbes*, March 14, 2017.

13. Fred Walumbwa, Bruce Avolio, William Gardner, Tara Wernsing, and Suzanne Peterson, "Authentic Leadership: Development and Validation of a Theory-Based Measure," *Journal of Management* 34, no. 1 (February 2008): 89–126.

14. Rachel Clapp-Smith, Gretchen Vogelgesang, and James Avey, "Authentic Leadership and Positive Psychological Capital: The Mediating Role of Trust at the Group Level of Analysis," *Journal of Leadership and Organizational Studies* 15, no. 3 (February 2009): 227–40.

15. Erik de Haan, Vicki Culpin, and Judy Curd, "Executive Coaching in Practice: What Determines Helpfulness for Clients of Coaching?" *Personnel Review* 40, no. 1 (2011): 24–44.

16. Y. Joel Wong, "The Psychology of Encouragement: Theory, Research, and Applications," *Counseling Psychologist* 43, no. 2 (2015): 178–216.

## Chapter 4: Team First

1. Charles Darwin, *Descent of Man, and Selection in Relation to Sex* (London: J. Murray, 1871), 166.

2. James W. Pennebaker, *The Secret Life of Pronouns: What Our Words Say About Us* (New York: Bloomsbury, 2011).

3. Carol S. Dweck, *Mindset: The New Psychology of Success* (New York: Random House, 2006), 7.

4. Daniel J. McAllister, "Affect- and Cognition-Based Trust as Foundations for Interpersonal Cooperation in Organizations," *Academy of Management Journal* 38, no. 1 (1995): 24–59.

5. U.S. Equal Employment Opportunity Commission, *Diversity in High Tech*, May 2016; Elena Sigacheva, *Quantifying the Gender Gap in Technology*, Entelo, March 8, 2018, blog.entelo.com.

6. Anita Williams Woolley, Christopher F. Chabris, Alex Pentland, Nada Hashmi, and Thomas W. Malone, "Evidence for a Collective Intelligence Factor in the Performance of Human Groups," *Science* 330, no. 6004 (October 2010): 686–88.

7. Laura Sherbin and Ripa Rashid, "Diversity Doesn't Stick Without Inclusion," *Harvard Business Review*, February 1, 2017.

8. A good exploration of these two approaches to coping with "stressors" can be found here: Charles S. Carver, Michael F. Scheier, and Jagdish Kumari Weintraub, "Assessing Coping Strategies: A Theoretically Based Approach," *Journal of Personality and Social Psychology* 56, no. 2 (February 1989): 267–83.

9. Alice M. Isen, Kimberly A. Daubman, and Gary P. Nowicki, "Positive Affect Facilitates Creative Problem Solving," *Journal of Personality and Social Psychology* 52, no. 6 (June 1987): 1122–31.

10. Kaplan, *Startup*, 254.

11. Walter F. Baile, Robert Buckman, Renato Lenzi, Gary Glober, Estela A. Beale, and Andrzej P. Kudelka, "SPIKES—A Six-Step Protocol for Delivering Bad News: Application to the Patient with Cancer," *Oncologist* 5, no. 4 (August 2000): 302–11.

12. John Gerzema and Michael D'Antonio, *The Athena Doctrine: How Women (and the Men Who Think Like Them) Will Rule the Future* (San Francisco: Jossey-Bass, 2013).

## Chapter 5: The Power of Love

1. Nicolas O. Kervyn, Charles M. Judd, and Vincent Y. Yzerbyt, "You Want to Appear Competent? Be Mean! You Want to Appear Sociable? Be Lazy! Group Differentiation and the Compensation Effect," *Journal of Experimental Social Psychology* 45, no. 2 (February 2009): 363–67.

2. Kaplan, *Startup*, 42.

3. Sigal G. Barsade and Olivia A. O'Neill, "What's Love Got to Do with It? A Longitudinal Study of the Culture of Companionate Love and Employee and Client Outcomes in a Long-term Care Setting," *Administrative Science Quarterly* 59, no. 4 (November 2014): 551–98.

4. Suzanne Taylor, Kathy Schroeder, and John Doerr, *Inside Intuit: How the Makers of Quicken Beat Microsoft and Revolutionized an Entire Industry* (Boston: Harvard Business Review Press, 2003), 231.

5. Jason M. Kanov, Sally Maitlis, Monica C. Worline, Jane E. Dutton, Peter J. Frost, and Jacoba M. Lilius, "Compassion in Organizational Life," *American Behavioral Scientist* 47, no. 6 (February 2004): 808–27.

6. This 1999 paper from Duke University explores the concept of social capital in depth: Nan Lin, "Building a Network Theory of Social Capital," *Connections* 22, no. 1 (1999): 28–51.

7. Adam Grant, *Give and Take: Why Helping Others Drives Our Success* (New York: Penguin Books, 2013), 264–65.

8. Adam Grant and Reb Rebele, "Beat Generosity Burnout," *Harvard Business Review*, January 2017.

9. Brad Stone, *The Everything Store: Jeff Bezos and the Age of Amazon* (New York: Little, Brown, 2013).

## Chapter 6: The Yardstick

1. Fiona Lee and Larissa Z. Tiedens, "Is It Lonely at the Top? The Independence and Interdependence of Power Holders," *Research in Organizational Behavior* 23 (2001): 43–91.

# Index

Jobs, Steve (*cont.*)
 return to Apple, 12–13, 13n,
  37, 136
 Super Bowl ad and, 8–9
 Super Bowl XIX and, 168–69
Johnson, Eric, 66, 122
Johnson, Ron, 193
Jung, Andrea, 132, 136
J. Walter Thompson, 7

Kamangar, Salar, 91, 91n
Kanov, Jason, 7n
Kaplan, Jerry, 44–45, 90–91, 143,
 156–57, 179–80
Kets de Vries, Manfred F. R.,
 63n
Khosla, Vinod, 82, 96
King Arthur round-table model,
 56
Kinser, Dave, and family, 12, 96,
 169
Kleiner Perkins, 10, 10n, 13, 177
knowledge commonality, 44
Kodacolor 200 film, 67
Kodak, 7–8, 36, 66–67, 66n, 122
Kordestani, Omid, 112, 115, 163
Kramer, Scotty, 4–5, 17
Kvamme, E. Floyd, 9

LaMacchia, John, 59, 59n
Lambeau Field, 183–84, 184n
Landry, Tom, 86
layoffs and firings, 71–72
leadership. *See also* managers and
 management
 authentic, 98–99
 disagreeable givers, 98–99
 first principles, based on, 57–60
 humility and, 86, 87–88, 88n
 listening and, 91
 management excellence and,
  35–37, 51

peer feedback survey and, 125,
 126
positive, 136–37
when things go wrong, 141–44
Lee, Fiona, 187n
Lilius, Jacoba, 7n
LinkedIn, 108n
listening, free-form, 89–92, 98
*Los Angeles Times*, 9
Lott, Ronnie, 15, 41
love, 155–84
 applause, percussive, 166–68
 "Billisms," top ten, 159
 building communities, 168–73
 caring about people, 160–65
 elevator chat, 181–82
 football and, 183–84
 of founders, 177–81
 helping people, 174–77
 hug-and-curses greetings,
  155–56
 warmth and competence,
  156–58
loyalty, 81, 139, 142, 143, 144,
 162
Lund University, 91

Macintosh computer, 8–9
Maitlis, Sally, 7n
managers and management,
 31–78. *See also* leadership
 aberrant geniuses and, 61–64
 boards, 73–77
 decision making, 52–57
 elimination of, 31–34
 first, 32n
 first principles and, 57–60
 framework for 1:1s and reviews,
  51
 "it's the people," 37–41
 layoffs and firings, 71–72
 leadership and, 35–37, 51

# About the Authors

ERIC SCHMIDT served as Google CEO and chairman from 2001 until 2011, Google executive chairman from 2011 to 2015, and Alphabet executive chairman from 2015 to 2018.

JONATHAN ROSENBERG is a senior vice president at Alphabet and an advisor to the company's management team. He ran the Google product team from 2002 to 2011.

ALAN EAGLE has been a director at Google since 2007. Formerly Eric and Jonathan's speechwriter, he currently runs a set of Google's sales programs.

Together, they are the authors of the bestselling book *How Google Works*.